Nellie Bly

Nellie Bly

ELIZABETH EHRLICH

CHELSEA HOUSE PUBLISHERS

NEW YORK • PHILADELPHIA

CHELSEA HOUSE PUBLISHERS
EDITOR-IN-CHIEF: Nancy Toff
EXECUTIVE EDITOR: Remmel T. Nunn
MANAGING EDITOR: Karyn Gullen Browne
COPY CHIEF: Juliann Barbato
PICTURE EDITOR: Adrian G. Allen
ART DIRECTOR: Maria Epes
MANUFACTURING MANAGER: Gerald Levine

American Women of Achievement
SENIOR EDITOR: Constance Jones

Staff for NELLIE BLY
ASSOCIATE EDITOR: Maria Behan
COPY EDITOR: Nicole Bowen
DEPUTY COPY CHIEF: Ellen Scordato
EDITORIAL ASSISTANT: Heather Lewis
PICTURE RESEARCHER: Susan Biederman
ASSISTANT ART DIRECTOR: Laurie Jewell
DESIGN: Design Oasis
DESIGNER: Donna Sinisgalli
PRODUCTION COORDINATOR: Joseph Romano
COVER ILLUSTRATOR: Maria Ruotolo

First Printing

1   3   5   7   9   8   6   4   2

Library of Congress Cataloging-in-Publication Data

Ehrlich, Elizabeth.
  Nellie Bly.

  (American women of achievement)
  Bibliography: p.
  Includes index.
  Summary: Follows the life of the celebrated reporter, from her
early days to her trip around the world and later triumphs.
  1. Bly, Nellie, 1867–1922.   2. Journalists—United States—
Biography.   [1. Bly, Nellie, 1867–1922.   2. Journalists]   I.
Title.   II. Series.
PN4874.C59E37   1989   070'.92'4 [B] [92]   88-34152
ISBN 1-55546-643-5
     0-7910-0428-7 (pbk.)

CONTENTS

AMERICAN WOMEN of ACHIEVEMENT

Abigail Adams
women's rights advocate

Jane Addams
social worker

Louisa May Alcott
author

Marian Anderson
singer

Susan B. Anthony
woman suffragist

Ethel Barrymore
actress

Clara Barton
*founder of the American
Red Cross*

Elizabeth Blackwell
physician

Nellie Bly
journalist

Margaret Bourke-White
photographer

Pearl Buck
author

Rachel Carson
biologist and author

Mary Cassatt
artist

Agnes De Mille
choreographer

Emily Dickinson
poet

Isadora Duncan
dancer

Amelia Earhart
aviator

Mary Baker Eddy
*founder of the Christian
Science church*

Betty Friedan
feminist

Althea Gibson
tennis champion

Emma Goldman
political activist

Helen Hayes
actress

Lillian Hellman
playwright

Katharine Hepburn
actress

Karen Horney
psychoanalyst

Anne Hutchinson
religious leader

Mahalia Jackson
gospel singer

Helen Keller
humanitarian

Jeane Kirkpatrick
diplomat

Emma Lazarus
poet

Clare Boothe Luce
author and diplomat

Barbara McClintock
biologist

Margaret Mead
anthropologist

Edna St. Vincent Millay
poet

Julia Morgan
architect

Grandma Moses
painter

Louise Nevelson
sculptor

Sandra Day O'Connor
Supreme Court justice

Georgia O'Keeffe
painter

Eleanor Roosevelt
diplomat and humanitarian

Wilma Rudolph
champion athlete

Florence Sabin
medical researcher

Beverly Sills
opera singer

Gertrude Stein
author

Gloria Steinem
feminist

Harriet Beecher Stowe
author and abolitionist

Mae West
entertainer

Edith Wharton
author

Phillis Wheatley
poet

Babe Didrikson Zaharias
champion athlete

CHELSEA HOUSE PUBLISHERS

"Remember the Ladies"

MATINA S. HORNER

Remember the Ladies." That is what Abigail Adams wrote to her husband John, then a delegate to the Continental Congress, as the Founding Fathers met in Philadelphia to form a new nation in March of 1776. "Be more generous and favorable to them than your ancestors. Do not put such unlimited power in the hands of the Husbands. If particular care and attention is not paid to the Ladies," Abigail Adams warned, "we are determined to foment a Rebellion, and will not hold ourselves bound by any Laws in which we have no voice, or Representation."

The words of Abigail Adams, one of the earliest American advocates of women's rights, were prophetic. Because when we have not "remembered the ladies," they have, by their words and deeds, reminded us so forcefully of the omission that we cannot fail to remember them. For the history of American women is as interesting and varied as the history of our nation as a whole. American women have played an integral part in founding, settling, and building our country. Some we remember as remarkable women who—against great odds—achieved distinction in the public arena: Anne Hutchinson, who in the 17th century became a charismatic religious leader; Phillis Wheatley, an 18th-century black slave who became a poet; Susan B. Anthony, whose name is synonymous with the 19th-century women's rights movement, and who led the struggle to enfranchise women; and, in our own century, Amelia Earhart, the first woman to cross the Atlantic Ocean by air.

These extraordinary women certainly merit our admiration, but other women, "common women," many of them all but forgotten, should also be recognized for their contributions to American thought and culture. Women have been community builders; they have founded schools and formed voluntary associations to help those in need; they have assumed the major responsibility for rearing children, passing on from one generation to the next the values that keep a culture alive. These and innumerable other contributions, once ignored, are now being recognized by scholars, students, and the public. It is exciting and gratifying to realize that a part of our history that was hardly acknowledged a few generations ago is now being studied and brought to light.

In recent decades, the field of women's history has grown from obscurity to a politically controversial splinter movement to academic respectability, in many cases mainstreamed into such traditional disciplines as history, economics, and psychology. Scholars of women, both female and male, have organized research centers at such prestigious institutions as Wellesley College, Stanford University, and the University of California. Other notable centers for women's studies are the Center for the American Woman and Politics at the Eagleton Institute of Politics at Rutgers University; the Henry A. Murray Research Center for the Study of Lives, at Radcliffe College; and the Women's Research and Education Institute, the research arm of the Congressional Caucus on Women's Issues. Other scholars and public figures have established archives and libraries, such as the Schlesinger Library on the History of Women in America, at Radcliffe College, and the Sophia Smith Collection, at Smith College, to collect and preserve the written and tangible legacies of women.

From the initial donation of the Women's Rights Collection in 1943, the Schlesinger Library grew to encompass vast collections documenting the manifold accomplishments of American women. Simultaneously, the women's movement in general and the academic discipline of women's studies in particular also began with a narrow definition and gradually expanded their mandate. Early causes such as woman suffrage and social reform, abolition and organized labor were joined by newer concerns such as the history of women in business and the professions and in politics and government; the study of the family; and social issues such as health policy and education.

Women, as historian Arthur M. Schlesinger, jr., once pointed out, "have constituted the most spectacular casualty of traditional history. They have made up at least half the human race, but you could never tell that by looking at the books historians write." The new breed of historians is remedying that omission. They have written books about immigrant women and about working-class women who struggled for survival in cities and about black women who met the challenges of life in rural areas. They are telling the stories of women who, despite the barriers of tradition and economics, became lawyers and doctors and public figures.

The women's studies movement has also led scholars to question traditional interpretations of their respective disciplines. For example, the study of war has traditionally been an exercise in military and political analysis, an examination of strategies planned and executed by men. But scholars of women's history have pointed out that wars have also been periods of tremendous change and even opportunity for women, because the very absence of men on the home front enabled them to expand their educational, economic, and professional activities and to assume leadership in their homes.

The early scholars of women's history showed a unique brand of courage in choosing to investigate new subjects and take new approaches to old ones. Often, like their subjects, they endured criticism and even ostracism by their academic colleagues. But their efforts have unquestionably been worthwhile, because with the publication of each new study and book another piece of the historical patchwork is sewn into place, revealing an increasingly comprehensive picture of the role of women in our rich and varied history.

Such books on groups of women are essential, but books that focus on the lives of individuals are equally indispensable. Biographies can be inspirational, offering their readers the example of people with vision who have looked outside themselves for their goals and have often struggled against great obstacles to achieve them. Marian Anderson, for instance, had to overcome racial bigotry in order to perfect her art and perform as a concert singer. Isadora Duncan defied the rules of classical dance to find true artistic freedom. Jane Addams had to break down society's notions of the proper role for women in order to create new social institutions, notably the settlement house. All of these women had to come to terms both with themselves and with the world in which they lived. Only then could they move ahead as pioneers in their chosen callings.

Biography can inspire not only by adulation but also by realism. It helps us to see not only the qualities in others that we hope to emulate, but also, perhaps, the weaknesses that made them "human." By helping us identify with the subject on a more personal level they help us to feel that we, too, can achieve such goals. We read about Eleanor Roosevelt, for instance, who occupied a unique and seemingly enviable position as the wife of the president. Yet we can sympathize with her inner dilemma: an inherently shy woman, she had to force herself to live a most public life in order to use her position to benefit others. We may not be able to imagine ourselves having the immense poetic talent of Emily Dickinson, but from her story we can understand the challenges faced by a creative woman who was expected to fulfill many family responsibilities. And though few of us will ever reach the level of athletic accomplishment displayed by Wilma Rudolph or Babe Zaharias, we can still appreciate their spirit, their overwhelming will to excel.

A biography is a multifaceted lens. It is first of all a magnification, the intimate examination of one particular life. But at the same time, it is a wide-angle lens, informing us about the world in which the subject lived. We come away from reading about one life knowing more about the social, political, and economic fabric of the time. It is for this reason, perhaps, that the great New England essayist Ralph Waldo Emerson wrote, in 1841, "There is properly no history: only biography." And it is also why biography, and particularly women's biography, will continue to fascinate writers and readers alike.

Nellie Bly

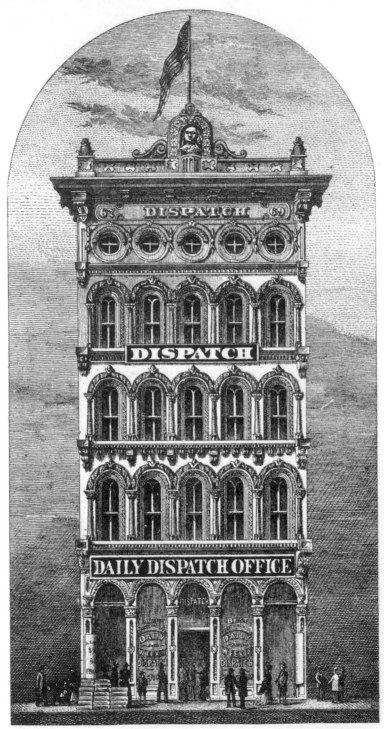

*Reporter Elizabeth Cochrane, who wrote under the pen
name Nellie Bly, began her career in the offices of
Pittsburgh, Pennsylvania's, most prominent newspaper,
the* Dispatch.

ONE

"Lonely Orphan Girl"

One morning in January 1885 an anonymous letter arrived at the office of the Pittsburgh *Dispatch*. It was addressed to the newspaper's editor, George Madden. Scrawled on a large sheet of paper, it looked like the sort of crank correspondence that a secretary might toss into a wastebasket unread.

Fortunately, though, Madden himself was looking over the mail that day. He was impressed by the mysterious letter, written by a correspondent who signed herself only "Lonely Orphan Girl." It was an angry yet eloquent response to an editorial that had appeared in the *Dispatch* as part of a regular feature called "Quiet Observations."

The "Quiet Observer" was a man named Erasmus Wilson, and his column was one of the newspaper's most popular features. The piece that had provoked the letter writer's wrath was entitled "What Girls Are Good For." Wilson's sarcastic editorial maintained that young women were "expensive luxuries" at home, troublesome interlopers when they went out to work. Females, he insisted, had no business moving into traditional male professions. They were unfit for "men's work," which, in Wilson's eyes, included basically all fields except teaching and nursing. The columnist went on to ridicule women who were striving for feminist ideals and new career opportunities.

While many readers may have chuckled over this piece, at least one did not. Twenty-one-year-old Elizabeth Cochrane immediately dashed off the indignant response that so impressed editor George Madden that January morning. The Quiet Observer,

Cochrane entered the male-dominated world of newspaper journalism in 1885. Her crusading spirit and impassioned style quickly won her a wide audience.

she wrote, had raised a serious question—"What shall we do with our girls?"—but had dealt with it frivolously. She pointed out that not all young women possess the money, beauty, or education that would help them make their way in life. Not all can marry; not all want to. Some have children to feed or aged parents dependent on them. Yet society chose to ignore these facts. There were hardly any occupations open to women, and these few did not pay well. Young women need work, Cochrane insisted—real jobs paying real wages.

Such sentiments were anything but commonplace in the 1880s, even though an increasing number of women were working outside the home to support themselves and their families. Since the end of the Civil War two decades before, a steady stream of poor and unskilled rural families had come to the cities, and every member had to pull his—or her—weight. During this same period, vast numbers of immigrants were flooding into the United States from Europe. These families, too, often depended on the earnings of their female members.

Upper-class women, for their part, were beginning to set their sights on expanded career opportunities and equal rights with men. A new suffragist movement, led by Susan B. Anthony and Elizabeth Cady Stanton, was demanding the vote for women. Many of these activists also advocated female employment as a way of ending women's economic dependence on men.

All this social ferment was extremely threatening to many. Perhaps some poor women had to work, but in the eyes of the middle and upper classes, these women were exceptions. It was unthinkable that a woman would seek employment unless she was driven by financial necessity, and to many, it seemed that the future of American families depended on women's staying home. Despite ample evidence to the contrary, women were idealized as being too delicate for the dirty world of daily labor outside the home.

Elizabeth Cochrane was well aware of the efforts of women such as Anthony to win increased opportunities for their sex. After her father died and her family's fortunes declined, she also grew to understand the plight of poor women who needed to work but could find little opportunity to do so. In her reply to the *Dispatch*'s editorial, Cochrane described her own fruitless job search, which had turned up nothing but low-paying kitchen work. Because of her delicate appearance, she was denied even those positions. Cochrane pointed out that although Wilson had mocked their plight, young women such as herself were growing desperate. The fields designated "women's

Columnist Erasmus Wilson penned the scathing editorial on women that prompted Cochrane's angry protest. Her letter brought her talents to the attention of the Dispatch.

Elizabeth Cady Stanton (left) and Susan B. Anthony meet in 1881 to plan the next stage in their battle to win the vote for women. Cochrane, an avid feminist, supported their efforts.

work" were all overcrowded. "The schools are overrun with teachers," she wrote, "the stores with clerks, the factories with employees. There are more cooks, chambermaids and washerwomen than can find employment."

The solution, Cochrane argued, was to open to women jobs traditionally held by men—and at the same pay. "It is asserted by storekeepers that women make the best clerks. Why not send them out as merchant travelers?" she asked. It was a radical idea. "This would be a good field for believers in woman's rights," she pointed out. "Take some girls that have the ability, procure for them situations. Pull them out of the mire and give them a shove up the ladder of life."

Editor Madden thoughtfully examined the letter. It was rough as far as style went. The writer did not seem to know what a paragraph was, and her sense of punctuation was equally vague. Nonetheless, he was intrigued by the author's conviction and spirit. He showed the letter to Erasmus Wilson, and the Quiet Observer was

Women toil in the sewing room of a clothing manufacturer. While searching for a job, Cochrane was discouraged to find that women were largely restricted to such poorly paid work.

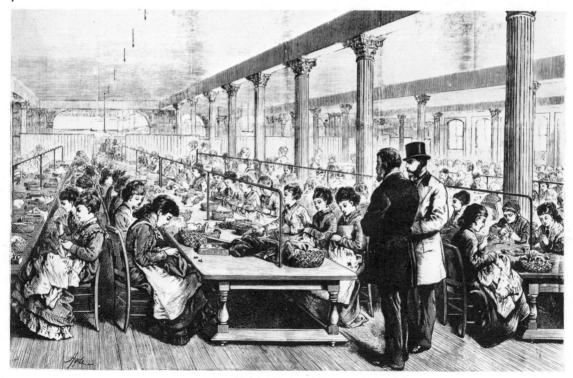

> a United States cent brought $200, a subscriber
> who has a United States half cent of 1904 in his
> possession would dispose of it if he only knew
> how. Would you be kind enough to inform me
> through the medium of your paper how and
> where, and oblige   A SUBSCRIBER.
> JANUARY 16, 1885.
>
> ─────────
>
> **Lonely Orphan Girl.**
> If the writer of the communication signed
> "Lonely Orphan Girl" will send her name and
> address to this office, merely as a guarantee of
> good faith, she will confer a favor and receive
> the information she desires.
>
> Lancaster Watch Factory Goes West.
> Special Telegram to the Dispatch.]
> LANCASTER, January 16.—The Lancaster
> Watch Company will be removed to Grand
> Crossing, four miles from Chicago, arrangements

After receiving Cochrane's eloquent rebuttal to the Dispatch's *editorial on women and work, Erasmus Wilson and editor George Madden ran this ad in their newspaper.*

equally impressed. The two of them decided to run an ad in the paper asking the writer to stop by so that they could meet her.

The afternoon the ad appeared, a gentle rap was heard at the door of the *Dispatch*'s editorial offices. "Come in!" shouted a brusque voice. The door opened quietly. In slipped a slight young woman dressed in a black silk dress, high-button shoes, and a small fur hat. With her large deep-set hazel eyes, reddish brown bangs curling at her forehead, and shy demeanor, Elizabeth Cochrane looked like a girl in her teens.

She stood at the office's threshold, observing the scene as she caught her breath after climbing four long flights of stairs. In 1885—and for many years afterward—newspaper offices were considered exclusively masculine domains. Newsrooms were messy, boisterous places that reeked of cigar smoke and the smell of printer's ink. Newsmen, something of a rakish breed, were known for their heavy drinking and salty language. Their talk, full of the politics, crime, and scandal that made for spicy newspaper copy, was thought far too worldly for the "dainty" female sex.

Elizabeth Cochrane knew that she was out of place in this environment. "I was awfully scared when I went to the office that first time," she later recalled. "I expected the managing editor to be a great big man with a bushy beard, who would look over the top of his specs and snap out, What d'ye want?' And the Quiet Observer I had pictured as a little gray-haired, sharp-nosed, sour-visaged chap who could look clean through you."

But Cochrane was determined to overcome any skepticism she might encounter. She was a young woman of extraordinary energy and determination —qualities that would be her trademarks throughout her lifetime. As the scene was later described in the *Dispatch*, she turned to the office boy, Willie, and announced, "I would like to see Mr. Madden."

"This is the gentleman," said Willie, gesturing to the managing editor.

Cochrane smiled for the first time

As this turn-of-the-century photo attests, newsrooms were exclusively male domains when Elizabeth Cochrane began her career in journalism.

since she had entered the newspaper office. "Oh! Is it?" she exclaimed. "I expected to see an old, cross man." Instead, she was face-to-face with a young, pleasant-looking one. "You asked me to call," she said to Madden.

"Oh yes, you are the girl who wrote the letter. All right, come into my office and we'll talk it over."

To the young woman's amazement, Madden offered to print her letter as an article and to pay her for it. He also offered her a job, beginning at once, at the rate of five dollars a week. It was a generous salary for a woman at that time—about twice as much as many female factory workers earned. Coch-

rane was thrilled by Madden's proposal and accepted at once.

Although the newsmen who witnessed her first timid foray into their lair would have scoffed at the idea, the *Dispatch*'s new employee would soon be its brightest star. In years to come, under the pen name Nellie Bly, she would become the best-known reporter in America. Righteous indignation, as expressed in her response to the Quiet Observer's insensitive column, had won her a job. And righteous indignation, as she fought for the poor, the uneducated, and the powerless, would propel her to the top of the newspaper field.

In her youth Elizabeth Cochran exhibited the dramatic flair that would be her lifelong trademark. As a teenager, she added the final e to her name as an elegant flourish.

TWO

Early Life

The girl who would grow up to be Nellie Bly was born Elizabeth Cochran on May 5, 1864, in Cochran's Mills, Pennsylvania. (As a teenager, Elizabeth added the final *e* to her last name, to give it an elegant touch.) This rural village was named after her father, Michael Cochran, the town's most prominent citizen. The Cochran family had an illustrious history. One of Michael Cochran's ancestors was a lord admiral of the British navy who won fame for his daring exploits. Elizabeth's great-grandfather Cochran settled in Maryland in colonial times. Convinced that the American colonies should break free of British rule, he helped pen a declaration of independence years before Thomas Jefferson composed the one that set the course of the American Revolution in 1776.

Elizabeth's family tree was equally extraordinary on her mother's side. Mary Jane Kennedy's clan had a strong streak of courage and independence. As a young man, Great-grandfather Kennedy had eloped with the daughter of a British nobleman and fled to America, where he served as an officer in the Revolutionary Army. A man of wealth, he eventually came to own almost all of Somerset County, Pennsylvania.

Of all Elizabeth's adventurous forebears, her grand-uncle Thomas Kennedy most intrigued her. During her childhood Elizabeth's imagination was fired by tales of Kennedy's adventures during a three-year trip around the world. The journey had been a grueling one. Uncle Thomas returned home in ruined health and never managed to

Elizabeth Cochran was born in this spacious Pennsylvania home on May 5, 1864.

write a book about his experiences, as he had intended. Inspired by her relative's example, Elizabeth would one day better his feat. Among her other achievements, she would set a new record for around-the-world travel—and produce a book about her journey—before her 26th birthday.

Elizabeth's father, Michael Cochran, was a man of action and ambition. He rose from his origins as a poor laborer to a position as a wealthy landowner who eventually served as justice of the peace and associate judge of Armstrong County. He was also a respected businessman who ran the general store and the post office. In addition, he owned the grist mill that employed many of the villagers.

Cochran had 10 children by his first wife. After her death, he married Mary Jane Kennedy, a widow. This marriage yielded five more children: three sons, Elizabeth, and one other daughter. Growing up in a household filled with youngsters, Elizabeth learned early on to hold her own. She possessed a flair for the dramatic and became the ringleader in the children's games despite being the second-youngest child—and a girl—in a predominantly male family.

In 1869 Judge Cochran gave up his store and mill and moved to the neighboring town of Apollo. There he began a thriving law practice and established his family in a large home. He had an extensive library and encouraged his children, including his daughters, to expand their horizons by reading. This attitude was unusual in an era when young girls were expected to learn little more than how to keep house. But Elizabeth would not benefit from her father's progressive influence for long. Michael Cochran died in 1870, when she was six years old.

Cochran left his family a substantial estate, and Elizabeth continued to grow up as an adored and pampered child. Her doting mother dressed her in starched and ruffled pink dresses. Pink, or Pinky, became the family's pet name for her. She was so small and delicate that some of the neighbors sadly predicted she would never grow up. But little Pink defied expectation by growing into a spirited, and occasionally stubborn, young girl. Accord-

This 19th-century photograph shows Cochran's Mills, Pennsylvania, where Elizabeth spent her first five years. The small town was named after her father, a wealthy businessman.

The Cochran family moved to the iron- and steel-manufacturing town of Apollo, Pennsylvania, (above) in 1869.

ing to Mignon Rittenhouse, the author of *The Amazing Nellie Bly*, young Elizabeth possessed a determination to "stand up to the boys." She met her older brothers' challenges whether they involved climbing trees, racing, or riding a horse while standing on its back. Elizabeth dreamed of faraway

places and the excitement of big cities, and she would often go to Apollo's railroad station to watch the trains that she imagined were bringing travelers to and from exotic destinations.

Mary Jane Kennedy Cochran, a strong and ambitious woman, encouraged Elizabeth to use her mind. But the education she gave her daughter was haphazard. At the age of 15, Elizabeth was sent to a fashionable boarding school in Indiana, Pennsylvania, but she returned home after less than a year because of ill health. Most of her studies took place at home, where she devoured her father's library and wrote fantastic stories inspired by the accounts she read.

One by one, Elizabeth's siblings left home and were married. Mary Jane Cochran eventually sold the house in Apollo, and she and her two daughters moved to Pittsburgh, where some of the Cochran children had settled. Elizabeth was then 20 years old, an age when women were expected to marry and start families. But she had little interest in following this course: The unconventional Elizabeth Cochrane longed for a career instead. She soon found, however, that there were few professions considered acceptable for women of her class. She could be a governess, or perhaps an elderly woman's companion. But such employment paid next to nothing and offered

Elizabeth Cochran was educated at home, except for an 1879 stint at the State Normal School, shown here. She left the Indiana, Pennsylvania, boarding school because of frail health.

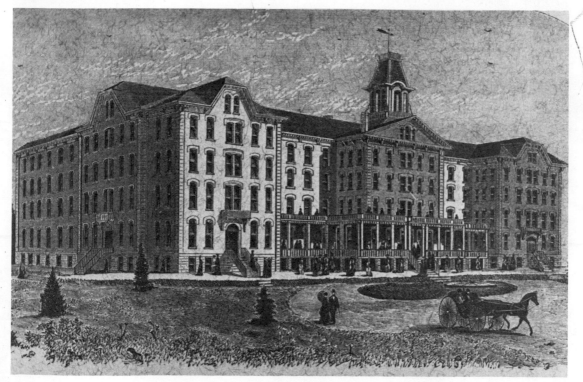

In 1884 Elizabeth Cochrane moved to the bustling city of Pittsburgh, Pennsylvania. The 20-year-old woman was eager to begin a writing career.

no hope of excitement or adventure.

Every morning Elizabeth Cochrane set out to scour the city for work; every evening she returned home dejected. Things grew desperate as Michael Cochran's legacy dwindled and she and her mother and sister were forced to move into increasingly shabby boarding houses. Unable to find a full-time job—and longing to become a professional writer—Elizabeth tried to sell free-lance articles, but her efforts met with no success. Then one fateful day she happened to see the Pittsburgh *Dispatch* editorial mocking the plight of young women who sought careers. By

the time she finished it, she was furiously angry. Riding the crest of that anger, she wrote the letter that started her on her way to fame and fortune as Nellie Bly, crusading reporter.

When Cochrane signed on at the Pittsburgh *Dispatch*, editor George Madden suggested that his new employee visit the places where women worked and write about them. Cochrane agreed, but asked that her first feature be on a different topic: divorce. It was a startling idea. In the 1880s divorce was considered to be a shameful scandal, something barely whispered about in polite society. It was not at all the sort of problem expected to concern a well-brought-up young woman.

Yet the subject was newsworthy. The incidence of divorce was increasing at an alarming rate. In Washington, Congress had just begun debating the merits of legislation regulating divorce, to replace a jumble of different laws on the books in each state. Even the issue of whether people should be allowed to divorce at all was still controversial. Some people felt it was only compassionate to allow unhappy couples to dissolve their marriages; others argued that sanctioning divorce would lead to a breakdown in religion, morality, and the general fabric of society.

Elizabeth Cochrane had a special interest in divorce because she had firsthand experience with the topic. Her mother had divorced her third husband, whom she had married after Michael Cochran's death. In an age that considered divorce unsavory, the divorce of Elizabeth's mother was truly shocking, for she, and not her husband, had filed for the divorce decree. To do so, she had been required by Pennsylvania law to appoint a guardian for her daughters, who were still minors at the time. Officially, then, Elizabeth Cochrane was an orphan, though her mother was still alive. Because of her curious legal status, Cochrane could honestly dub herself "Lonely Orphan Girl," as she did in the letter to the *Dispatch* that won her a job at the newspaper.

After considering Cochrane's idea, Madden told her to go ahead with the article on divorce. She put on her coat and left in a state of delight. Madden and his colleagues were surprisingly receptive to her ideas. "There wasn't an old cross man about the place," she remarked years later. "I was glad I was going to be a newspaper man."

This 19th-century cartoon shows the devil presiding over a divorce trial. Cochrane's first newspaper assignment tackled the controversial topic of divorce.

THREE

Nellie Bly, Reporter

Excited by the prospect of her first journalistic assignment, Elizabeth Cochrane took her seat on the streetcar. As she later reported in the *Dispatch*, she overheard two women chatting about one of their friends as the train trundled along. They spoke disapprovingly of their friend's new husband but concluded their scathing analysis by noting that the important thing, after all, was that she *did* get married.

Cochrane was appalled. Were women so afraid of remaining single that they would marry anyone at all? She certainly did not feel that way. "It is not all girls' missions to be wives any more than it is all men's to be husbands," she later remembered thinking. Clearly, attitudes such as the one she heard expressed on the streetcar contributed to the problem that

Cochrane was examining for the Pittsburgh *Dispatch*: divorce.

Several days after she embarked on the project, Cochrane handed her finished assignment to George Madden. Her first published piece, a polished version of her irate response to the newspaper's glib editorial on young women, had appeared in the *Dispatch* the week before. Headlined THE GIRL PUZZLE and signed "Lonely Orphan Girl," it had been a rousing success with the newspaper's readers. As he looked over the new article, Madden knew that the first piece had been no fluke. The story was a frank discussion of unhappy homes, brutal husbands, and unfaithful wives. Cochrane's writing style definitely needed improvement, especially in the grammar department. But Madden was im-

Combining demure elegance with a disregard for social convention, Elizabeth Cochrane was a paradox in the eyes of many who knew her.

pressed by the strong sentiments and powerful language that seemed to come instinctively to his new reporter.

Cochrane's piece was an impassioned plea. It called for reform of the marriage laws and recommended changes in individual behavior as well. Women, she maintained, should never marry simply out of the fear of becoming "old maids." They should choose their partners carefully, and if they are unable to find a suitable one, they should remain single. More prudent marriages, Cochrane pointed out, would help to eliminate the need for divorce.

She also insisted that it was unfair to look down on women who chose independence over marriage. "Women only ask justice," she wrote. "Men have been accustomed to looking on women as inferior beings in many ways. And now when women are realizing that all the happiness in the world does not arise from married life, and are trying to make a place for themselves, the selfish men would try to keep them back. But the day has passed when they can."

As he reached the end of the piece, Madden paused and looked up at Cochrane, who was anxiously awaiting his verdict on the article. Pen names were popular among journalists then. He wanted one for his newest reporter— something neat and catchy. As he tried to come up with a name, the story goes, Madden's assistant walked by, humming a tune. The song was "Nelly Bly," a popular air by the well-known Pittsburgh composer Stephen Foster. The lyrics had nothing to do with female reporters, but everyone knew the song. Madden thought that Nelly Bly would be a stylish and catchy moniker. But a typesetter's error intervened, and the first name was misspelled. From then on, Elizabeth Cochrane would be known to the world as Nellie Bly, reporter.

Nellie Bly's debut was a dramatic one. Headlined MAD MARRIAGES, her bold, sensitive article on divorce was the talk of Pittsburgh. Across the city,

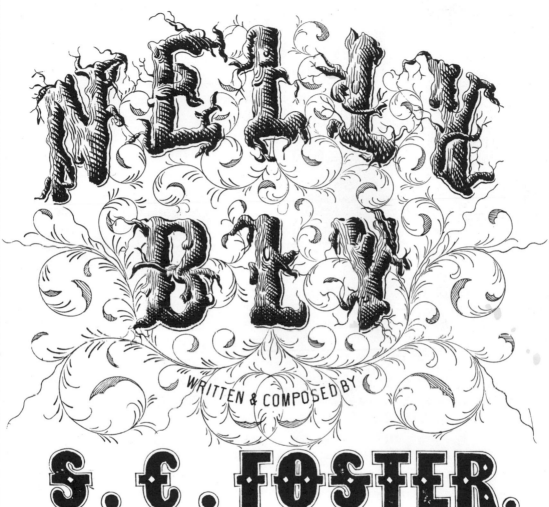

THIRTIETH EDITION

NELLY BLY

WRITTEN & COMPOSED BY

S. C. FOSTER.

PIANO ————————————————— GUITÁR

New York
PUBLISHED BY FIRTH. POND & C° N°547 BROADWAY.

Cincinnati. COLBURN & FIELD.   St. Louis: BALMER & WEBER.   Pittsburgh . H. KLEBER.

Entered according to Act of Congress A.D 1850 by Firth, Pond & C° in the Clerks Office of the dis.t Court of the South.n dis.t of N.Y.

In 1885 Elizabeth Cochrane became Nellie Bly. She adopted her pen name from a popular song by Pittsburgh composer Stephen Foster, the author of "O Susanna" and other well-known standards.

As a reporter for the Dispatch, *Nellie Bly interviewed prominent local industrialists such as Andrew Carnegie, pictured here. Her primary focus, however, was the city's poor workers.*

In the late 19th century Pittsburgh was a booming industrial center. Over half the nation's steel and a third of its glass were produced in or near the city. Andrew Carnegie, Henry Clay Frick, and others were building great business empires there. As these entrepreneurs prospered, the laboring classes flexed their muscles as well. Workers banded together to wrest some power from the factory owners, many of whom underpaid their employees and subjected them to poor, sometimes dangerous, working conditions. Newly formed unions fought for better wages, shorter hours, and safer workplaces. Collective bargaining, strikes, and picketing were the tools that the unions used to improve the lot of their members. Many business leaders resented the unions, however, and violence between union and antiunion forces broke out frequently. In 1892, for example, a strike against the Carnegie Steel Company resulted in several deaths.

Many of Pittsburgh's factories were "manned" by women, and it was these factories that Bly planned to write about next. Female workers faced the same challenges as men—and a host of additional problems. Like their male counterparts, they often worked 12- or 14-hour days for low wages under adverse conditions. But despite the hardships they faced, women were largely ignored by unions. Some male union members considered female employ-

people speculated about the identity of the *Dispatch*'s daring new reporter. Because of her strong opinions and fearless language, some suspected that a male writer was hiding behind a feminine *nom de plume*. Others thought that she must be a well-known feminist leader. George Madden and his staff played up the mystery, knowing that it would sell newspapers. Meanwhile, Nellie Bly went about her work.

Women use sharp tools in a pen factory's slitting room. Bly visited dozens of Pittsburgh establishments for her newspaper series on working women, often uncovering dangerous conditions.

ment a temporary "problem" that would be solved when they could afford to keep their wives and daughters out of the factories. Others feared that because women were paid one-third to one-half of men's wages, women might take jobs away from men. In fact, however, this seldom happened. The world of work was strictly sex segregated, and women were usually hired only for the least skilled jobs.

Elizabeth Cochrane was well aware of the limitations placed on working women. Before she won her job at the *Dispatch*, she herself had unsuccessfully tried to find a good job at decent wages. In her new guise as reporter Nellie Bly, she now set out to observe

women at work—and share her findings with her readers.

Bly went to dozens of factories, examining working conditions and meeting with laborers to discuss the rewards and pitfalls of their jobs. She visited women at work making hinges, cigars, shoes, and bread. Bly examined the products of their labors and spoke to their managers. She was accompanied on these visits by an artist, who made sketches and woodcuts of the workers. During the next few months her illustrated series, "Our Workshop Girls," had prominent play on the *Dispatch*'s Sunday feature page.

Bly's articles expressed pride at the achievements of the "workshop girls."

She painted them as heroines who were opening the way for women to live on their own, independent of parents or husbands. At most of the establishments she visited, she judged the work hard but the pay fair and the workers generally cheerful. Most women, of course, worked out of necessity, but many also prized the independence their pay gave them. At a yeast-packing factory, for instance, one laborer told Bly how much she detested housework. She insisted that she would never marry until she found a man wealthy enough to hire a maid. "Or," she said, "I'll let him stay at home and I'll take the man's place." Bly quoted these and other remarks in her articles, which brought the determination and exuberance of working women to the attention of the American public as never before.

But Bly's investigations also revealed a darker side of factory life. As she learned more about the lives of the city's female laborers, she realized that she had the makings not just of a series of articles but of a crusade. She informed her readers that young children were falling victim to unscrupulous employers who forced them to work long hours for slave wages, often at the expense of their health. Bly visited a tin factory where workers were fined for being a minute late, for speaking to other employees, and for endless other infractions. By payday, employees usually found that all their wages had been swallowed up by these penalties. According to one of Bly's pieces, one of the workers asked her: "Now what do you think of a man who pretends to be religious, who goes to church, has every comfort and even elegance at home, who rides in his carriage, and will then treat his girls so mean and fine them for everything, so as to get back their hard-earned two or three dollars?" Bly did not think much of such a man. After her impassioned article on the tin factory appeared in the Pittsburgh *Dispatch*, many of her readers shared her opinion.

Bly searched out establishments where working conditions were unwholesome, and she discovered that there were plenty. At a factory that prepared and bottled jellies, pickles, and relishes, she found the work not only unpleasant but dangerous and unsanitary as well. The women worked from early morning until late at night for barely enough money to survive. A bottle washer's hands and face could easily be scalded by the boiling hot water that splashed in the sinks. The hot, soapy bottles often slipped from fast-moving fingers, and workers frequently cut themselves on broken glass. On top of everything else, the factory was infested with rats.

Bly chronicled these and other abuses in illustrated features for the *Dispatch*. As she continued her investigations, she discovered that some factories would not admit reporters. In

Four seamstresses practice their trade. Bly's interviews with female workers revealed that many valued the independence their paychecks brought them, even if their daily jobs were tedious.

order to continue her work, Bly began experimenting with a bold new reporting style. To truly see what her subjects' lives were like, she would disguise herself and try living those lives, for a few hours at least. Then she could write from direct experience.

Some say that Bly got the idea from Erasmus Wilson. The Quiet Observer, whose column so angered her once, had become her mentor and would be

her friend for life. Far from the sour little man she had envisioned before she met him, she found Wilson to be a "great big good natured fellow who wouldn't even kill the cockroaches that crawled over his desk." Wilson was 20 years older than she, and married, but Bly had a crush on him that lasted for years.

Whatever its source, the "I was there" technique became Nellie Bly's

A tyrannical supervisor berates an employee. By working in factories, Bly discovered many abuses, including overseers who threatened or sexually harassed employees.

trademark. For her first undercover investigation she dressed in rough clothes and applied for a job in a basement workshop that made copper cables. Once hired, she learned how to twist lengths of copper wire into strong cords used for construction. It was hard, tedious work executed under the watchful eyes of a foreman who continually urged his harried workers to move faster. After just an hour on the job, Bly's back ached from bending over the cables, her hands were raw, and her eyes hurt from straining to see in the factory's dim light. She had worked up a terrible thirst as well and was appalled to learn that she needed permission simply to pause for a drink of water. Bly's description of her day in

the cable factory was graphic. Her readers, many of them for the first time, realized the toll that poor working conditions can take on laborers.

In the following weeks Bly expanded the scope of her articles, giving her readers shocking insights into the hardship and misery that took place daily in their city. She visited the slums where many of the laborers lived. She found people living in conditions beyond her worst imagination. Overcrowding and unsanitary conditions in the city's tenements bred crime, disease, and despair. Bly's sympathetic pieces helped her readers understand the thousands of women and men who had no choice but to raise their families in an unhealthy and dangerous environment. She also interviewed the public officials who she believed were largely responsible for the plight of the city's poor. Incensed by what she learned, she spared no blame and called loudly for reform.

Bly found that supposedly progressive public officials were ignoring abuses; others were powerless to stop them because there were no laws prohibiting them, as was the case with child labor. Her reports made many of her upper- and middle-class readers uncomfortable, reminding them that they had shirked their civic duty by ignoring the plight of poor workers. To Pittsburgh's laborers, Nellie Bly was the ardent champion they had long awaited. They respected a woman who took the trouble to discover what their lives were like by stepping into their shoes.

Bly's columns provoked citywide controversy. At the *Dispatch*, letters piled up from religious leaders, business people, politicians, trade unionists, women suffragists, and workers. Some complained about the newspaper's meddling "lady reporter"; others applauded her work and begged her to continue. Her articles did just what her critics feared and her admirers hoped: They sparked change. Public meetings were called to examine labor and housing problems, and slumlords and unscrupulous business owners were put on the defensive. Bly was especially gratified to learn that the sponsors of a state bill to limit the working hours of children used her articles to support their case.

Within only a few months, Nellie Bly had become one of Pittsburgh's best-known journalists. Her colleagues invited her to join the Pittsburgh Press Club, a unique honor for a woman. Her mailbox was always filled with letters that ranged from threats to marriage proposals. She had not yet reached her 22nd birthday, yet she was one of the most important people in the city.

George Madden began to have some misgivings about his crusading reporter, who frequented the most dangerous areas of town in order to do her job. According to Iris Noble, the author of *Nellie Bly*, Madden was worried

Nellie Bly visited many poor working women at home. She found that they often inhabited dilapidated slum dwellings such as the one pictured here.

Boys toil in a cotton mill. Bly's impassioned articles not only made her immensely popular with readers, they also spurred reform, including restrictions on child labor in Pennsylvania.

about more than Bly's safety: Powerful forces in business and politics had threatened to stop advertising in the *Dispatch* and to boycott the paper. They would only be satisfied if Bly stopped her investigations. Whatever his reasons, Madden abruptly decided that Nellie Bly's series on working women was finished.

Undaunted, the reporter turned her considerable energies to other projects. She interviewed the celebrities of the day, from wealthy Pittsburgh industrialist Andrew Carnegie to poet James Whitcomb Riley. Bly visited the new Western Penitentiary, the most modern prison of its day. Many readers found the idea of a woman visiting a prison filled with male criminals shocking, but she insisted on getting her story. She wrote approvingly of the humane conditions she found at the institution. Bly was especially pleased by the staff's efforts to rehabilitate the men by teaching them a trade. She pointed out that cruelty was commonplace at most other penal institutions and asserted that this was both immoral and counterproductive.

Increasingly, because of pressure from Madden, Bly's stories veered away from serious subjects. She often found herself limited to the standard topics assigned to the few "lady reporters" working in those days: fashion, society, the arts, cookery. She wrote articles on lace handkerchiefs, tree planting, theater, house pets, and the guests at the annual flower show. As the months dragged on, she began to find her assignments detestable and dull.

Nellie Bly longed for a challenge, something that no other young woman had ever done before. She kept her eyes open for opportunities. Then, one day toward the end of 1886 a diplomatic delegation from Mexico arrived in Pittsburgh, and Bly was asked to accompany the visitors as a member of the entertainment committee. Although Bly spoke no Spanish and the Mexicans knew little English, she managed to write some exceptionally well informed articles for the *Dispatch*. So impressed were the visitors that they invited the young reporter to visit their country. Nellie Bly had found the opportunity she had been waiting for. Although she knew she would face opposition, she made up her mind to go to Mexico.

Feeling confined by her role as the Dispatch's "lady reporter," Nellie Bly persuaded her editor to send her to Mexico. She planned to profile that nation's political scene and social climate.

FOUR

Adventures in Mexico

Nellie Bly presented her proposal to George Madden. As a foreign correspondent, she argued, she could bring the realities of Mexico to the readers of the Pittsburgh *Dispatch*. She would travel around the nation, reporting on the political scene, the people, and the countryside.

Bly saw the trip as an ideal vehicle for an inquiring reporter—and the perfect antidote to cold, workaday Pittsburgh and the dull assignments she was pursuing there. Mexico represented sun, romance, adventure. The country, it was said, had changed considerably since the overthrow of Emperor Maximilian two decades before. But little, really, was known about Mexico in the United States. Bly hoped to change that.

George Madden tried to dissuade her from undertaking her scheme. He

had worried when Bly roamed Pittsburgh's slums unescorted; he dreaded the idea of her traveling through Mexico alone. The editor had heard that the country was plagued by political instability, unscrupulous adventurers, and desperate bandits. He voiced his fears to Bly, but she refused to abandon her idea. Finally, Madden knew he was beaten. He authorized expense money for the trip and warned her to be careful. But he need not have worried about his daring reporter. Nellie Bly was equal to any challenge.

Bly eagerly prepared for her Mexican adventure. She asked her mother to join her on the journey, and Mary Jane Cochran agreed—probably in order to keep an eye on her intrepid daughter. As winter set in and 1886 drew to a close, the 21-year-old Bly said her farewells to her friends,

Bly, who had never before been outside Pennsylvania, was enchanted by the people and sights she glimpsed on her long train journey, especially the rugged cowboys of the American West.

donned a smart new traveling costume, and set off on the night train heading west. She had never before been outside Pennsylvania, and she was thrilled to be on her way.

As her train moved west and south, Bly was elated by the changing scenery. She was especially taken by the open skies and dramatic landscape of the western United States. The snow and cold and the crowded, dirty cities of the East seemed far away. "For a moment it seemed a dream," she wrote. "The trees were in leaf and the balmy breezes mocked our wraps."

For the first time, Bly was seeing the vast American continent and its people. She saw lush forests, rolling hills, and flat plains that stretched as far as the eye could see. The cotton fields, ruffled by breezes, made her think of billowing white sea foam. But she was more concerned with social issues than scenery. Bly marveled at the sight of "gaunt, tired women plowing the fields, while their lords and masters sat on the fences and smoked." She told her readers back home that "I never longed for anything so much as I did to shove those lazy fellows off."

She was more impressed with the West's hardworking cowboys, with their ten-gallon hats, spurs, lassos, and rugged way of life. Once, as she passed through the western plains, Bly spotted two horsemen. She waved a red scarf at them in greeting. To her delight, they doffed their hats and took off at a breakneck gallop in order to ride alongside her train. "I never felt as much reluctance for leaving a man behind me as I did to leave those cowboys," she informed her readers back in Pittsburgh.

On the third day of the journey Bly's sleep was disturbed by a predawn wake-up call. The train was approaching El Paso, Texas, a city on the Mexican border. The porter's call was most unwelcome to Bly, a lifelong night owl who preferred to go to bed at dawn than to rise at that hour. As she later related in her book *Six Months in Mexico*, she wished, just for a moment, that she had stayed comfortably at home. Bly rubbed her eyes and quickly dressed in the sleeping compartment she shared with her mother.

"It's so dark," Mrs. Cochran said, peering worriedly through the curtains. "What shall we do when we arrive?"

"Well, I'm glad it's dark," her daughter responded, trying to cheer them both up. "I won't have to button my boots or comb my hair."

Bly hardly felt cheerful a few minutes later, however, when she and her mother found themselves standing on a dark platform in a strange city. Porters rushed past them swinging oil lamps, ignoring the tired passengers picking their way around piles of freight and baggage. The waiting room was gloomy and depressing, filled with women, children, men, dogs, and the sickening smells of smoke and stale food. A group of men passed around a liquor bottle as they whiled away the time with a card game. Bly and her

Traveling through the farm belt during her 1886 train trip to Mexico, Bly noticed that many women performed heavy labor while "their lords and masters sat on the fences and smoked."

mother were exhausted, the train for Mexico was not leaving until that afternoon, and El Paso's hotels were all closed at that hour.

"This has taught me a lesson," Bly grimly joked. "I shall fall into the arms of the first man who mentions marriage to me. Then I shall have someone to look after me."

The reporter's spirits flagged only for a moment before she pulled herself together to remedy the situation. After talking to several people, she managed to arrange for a room with the family of a railroad employee. That evening she and her mother finally crossed the Mexican border.

To make her traveling allowance go further, she convinced three Mexican railroad companies to give her and her mother free passage. They began to travel extensively. Bly visited small villages and big towns, sending reports back to the *Dispatch*.

Bly gave her readers an overview of America's little-known neighbor. She

A man and his son plow the fields in the Mexican countryside. To report on the country for her readers back home, Bly traveled extensively, visiting large cities and rural towns alike.

This cathedral was one of the stately buildings that impressed Bly during her stay in Mexico City. She made the nation's capital her headquarters during her six months in the country.

rhapsodized over the country's picturesque landscapes: "How I would like to show you the green valley where the heat of summer and blast of winter never dare approach; where every foot of ground recalls wonderful historical events." Pieces on Mexican agriculture, archaeology, and culture also found their way to her Pittsburgh audience. After Bly attended a bullfight in Veracruz, she reported that she admired the toreador's costumes but pitied the bull.

During her sojourn Bly's home base was Mexico City, the nation's capital. She praised its beautiful avenues, lined with stately buildings and elegant shops. She visited the city's churches and museums. During her stay, Bly became acquainted with the popular American poet Joaquin Miller, then writing in Mexico. Impressed by both her curiosity and her bravery, he dubbed her "Little Nell, a second Columbus."

Back home, the *Dispatch*'s editors had the unenviable task of working with the copy Bly posted as she traveled. Her reports were filled with facts, wit, and fine observations. But they were carelessly scrawled in pencil, and sometimes periods and commas

A bull charges a matador at a Mexican bullfight. In one of her travel articles, Bly characterized these contests as barbaric yet colorful.

were forgotten as Bly enthusiastically dashed off her impressions and thoughts.

Once her work was edited and in print, though, Nellie Bly's progress was avidly followed by her hometown readers. Newspapers across the country printed her reports. Aided by a growing knowledge of Spanish, she garnered information and anecdotes that were considered exotic, even risqué, in 1886. Readers learned of "The Coffee House of the Little Hell" and a grocery store called "Tail of the Devil." Bly even sent home some Mexican recipes. "Of course you will think them horrible at first," she allowed. "But once you acquire the taste, American food is insipid by comparison."

But as she had been back in Pittsburgh, the *Dispatch*'s star reporter was most interested in people. Her vivid writing exposed Americans to the women, men, and children of Mexico: mothers carrying babies on their backs in colorful woven shawls, laundresses toting piles of neatly folded linens, tortilla makers hawking their goods in squares, and water carriers making their way down crowded streets. Her readers learned of the gala Sunday promenades that took place in many of the country's urban parks. She described exotically beautiful women as well as their handsome suitors, who paraded grandly on horseback in the hope of catching their favorite's eye.

Bly did not let her enjoyment of such scenes blind her to the social injustice that existed in the country. She contrasted "the elegants of Mexico City," who sported the latest Parisian fashions, with the city's street dwellers—the poorest of the poor. "They never repose," she wrote of them, "but sit with heads on their knees. When they are hungry they eat what they have scraped together during the day; spoiled meat and scraps boiled over a handful of charcoal. . . . They are worse off by thousands of times than were the slaves of the United States."

Bly was also sharply critical of the Mexican government. She bitterly remarked that Mexico was "a republic only in name, being in reality the worst monarchy in existence." She considered many of the country's politicians unprincipled and corrupt and felt sure that election fraud was commonplace. She also concluded that most of the Mexican press was controlled by the state. "Mexican papers," she charged, "never publish one word against the government or officials."

As a feminist, Bly was disappointed by the status of the nation's women. In her opinion, the situation had been bad in the United States; in Mexico, she found it even worse. It seemed to her that Mexican women were enslaved by their husbands, with practically no opportunity to earn an honest living on their own. Women were ex-

pected to do nothing but devote their lives to the domestic comfort of their families. They were suspect if they even ventured onto the street.

Bly learned this lesson the hard way one day when she found herself the only female on a mule-drawn streetcar in the city of Veracruz. The male passengers, she reported, looked at her with suspicion and disgust. But, as she wrote her readers back home, she refused to be cowed: "I defied the gaze of the passengers and showed them that a free American girl can accommodate herself to any circumstances without the aid of a man."

Most of Bly's blistering attacks were

Upper-class Mexican señoritas sport veils and fans for a day's outing. Bly poked good-natured fun at the country's high society, just as she had done with America's upper classes.

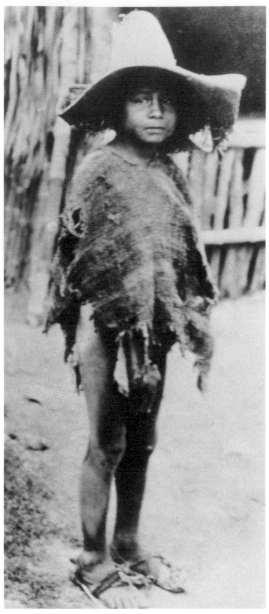

A young boy stands outside his family's shack. The plight of Mexico's poor captured Bly's attention during her stay there and became a primary focus for her articles.

written once she returned to the United States in 1887. While she remained south of the border, she tempered her criticisms. She knew that Mexican journalists had been imprisoned and even killed for speaking out against the government. Foreigners, too, were discouraged from freely expressing their opinions. "I had some regard for my health," Bly wrote after her return, "and a Mexican jail is the least desirable abode on the face of the earth, so some care was exercised in the selection of topics while we were inside their gates."

Careful as she was to appease the Mexican authorities while she remained in their country, she did send one openly critical dispatch during her trip. The story, concerning some newspaper editors who had been jailed, was widely reprinted in the United States. Eventually, the item reached Mexico, and the authorities were far from pleased. Bly received an anonymous note saying, "One button is enough." She interpreted this cryptic note as meaning that "by one article the officials could see what my others were like." She decided it was time to leave the country. The intrepid reporter managed to smuggle out a suitcase filled with notes by telling Mexican customs agents that it contained "ladies unmentionables." Embarrassed, they waved her through without searching her bag.

Bly wrote that the poor of Mexico "are worse off by thousands of times than were the slaves of the United States."

Bly and her mother returned to Pittsburgh in the spring of 1887. The *Dispatch* welcomed her back. Madden congratulated her on her successes in Mexico and raised her salary to $15 a week. After her travels, though, Pittsburgh seemed small and dull. She was dissatisfied with her assignments on the *Dispatch* and battled constantly with the city editor. She now saw Pittsburgh as a backwater, especially in the newspaper world. To grow further in her profession, to achieve real fame, she had to move on.

It did not take Bly long to make her decision. One day, within a few months of her return from Mexico, she simply failed to show up at the office. No one knew where she was until Erasmus Wilson found the following note on his desk:

Dear Quiet Observer—
I am off for New York. Look out for your naughty kid,
                                   Nellie Bly.

Shoppers and peddlers throng the streets of lower Manhattan. Finding Pittsburgh tame after her adventurous foray into Mexico, Nellie Bly moved to New York City in 1887.

FIVE

New York

The summer of 1887 was stiflingly hot in New York. The newspapers were filled with advertisements for resort hotels in the mountains or by the ocean. Those who could get away from the steamy city left town. But even during this sweltering summer New York still bustled with activity.

The city served as the United States's great port of entry. Immigrants from all over Europe flooded through its gates, bringing diverse languages and traditions as well as the vigor and determination to succeed in their new land. The streets were thronged with peddlers and pushcarts; the tenements overflowed with the poor and struggling. Most of the city's residents had been drawn there by the opportunities that New York offered as a commercial center, and indeed, many were making their fortunes there. With the fruit of their labors, new millionaires were building elaborate mansions on Fifth Avenue. New York was an exciting city, and Nellie Bly was ready for new challenges

Like millions of others, 23-year-old Nellie Bly arrived in the city with high hopes for the future. She rented a furnished room for herself and her mother and began to look for work. Bly wrote a few pieces for some of the city's newspaper syndicates and completed *Six Months in Mexico*, a book on her recent journey. But her primary goal was to win a job at one of New York's high-powered newspapers.

When Bly moved there, New York was the center of the journalistic world. A half-dozen prominent papers competed for readers, using dramatic headlines, pictures, features—every gimmick their editors could dream up.

Newsboys pick up their wares before dispersing across New York. When Bly arrived there to build a career, the city was the center of American journalism.

Bly familiarized herself with all of the city's major publications—the *Tribune*, the *Sun*, the *Times*—and wrote to their editors asking for employment.

It did not take her long, however, to fix on one particular newspaper as her primary target. The most exciting sheet in town was the New York *World*. Joseph Pulitzer, whose name is now synonymous with ground-breaking journalism, had recently bought the paper from wealthy financier Jay Gould. Under Gould, the *World* had

been a miserable failure. But Pulitzer, who had bucked the odds so often in his career, was turning the paper around magnificently. His formula for success included long stories, big headlines, cartoons, illustrations, and sensationalistic crime coverage. His methods were extraordinarily successful. By 1887 the *World*'s circulation was 200,000 a day—twice as large as any other morning paper's.

When he immigrated to the United States from Hungary, Pulitzer was a penniless teenager who spoke no English. He arrived during the Civil War, joined the Union cavalry, then worked odd jobs in St. Louis after the conflict ended. His ambition and drive were immense. While still a young man, he became the publisher of the St. Louis *Post-Dispatch*, one of the biggest newspapers in America at the time. He went on to serve a term in the Missouri legislature and then returned to the newspaper business.

As publisher of the *World*, Pulitzer was not just interested in printing the best writing and biggest scoops: He was looking for exposés, features, and investigative work that would promote positive social change. He wanted the *World* to be the newspaper of workers, not of the rich. After Pulitzer took over, he had the publication's philosophy printed on the masthead of every paper. The *World*, it proclaimed, would "always fight for progress and reform, never tolerate injustice or corruption, always oppose privileged classes and public plunderers, never lack sympathy with the poor, always remain devoted to the public welfare—not just for a day, not just for a year, but always."

After Bly arrived in New York, she noted with approval that the *World* was publishing reports on unhealthy conditions at local dairies and on the wretched lot of the nation's coal miners. The paper also took an unusually strong position against racial discrim-

This cartoon depicts the phenomenal rise in the New York World*'s circulation after publisher Joseph Pulitzer bought the paper in 1863.*

ination, and it looked critically at New York's jails and public bathhouses, exhorting city officials to improve them. Such adversarial journalism was still quite new. But it was just the type of writing that Nellie Bly did best. She wrote to Pulitzer, asking him to give her a trial run by sending her up in the hot-air balloon he was sponsoring at the St. Louis World's Fair. Bly hoped that he would hire her as a staff reporter if her liked her article on the balloon ride.

New York City tenement dwellers sleep outside to escape the summer heat. Pulitzer's World *championed the city's poor, and this concern attracted Bly to the popular newspaper.*

But Pulitzer and the *World* ignored her. So did the rest of the city's newspaper community. Here in New York, Nellie Bly was an unknown. Her Pittsburgh reputation cut no ice. The second strike against her was her sex. No one, it seemed, had any use for a woman journalist, even one with proven abilities. Toward the end of the

summer the young journalist hit bottom when her purse was stolen. It contained $100, nearly all the money she had left. Too proud to ask her friends for help, she resolved to make a last-ditch attempt to secure a job at the New York *World*.

Bly sat down and listed half a dozen ideas for innovative stories. She put on a thumb ring she wore for luck and made her way to Park Row, the center of New York's newspaper industry. With no introduction or appointment, she marched into the gold-domed *World* building and told the lobby guard that she wanted to see Mr. Pulitzer. The guard told her what he would say to any upstart who insisted on seeing the publisher: Mr. Pulitzer was not receiving visitors.

For three hours Bly stood her ground, arguing with various employees and refusing to take no for an answer. Finally she wore them out. She was shown into the inner sanctum—the offices of Pulitzer and his managing editor, John A. Cockerill. The two men received her reluctantly, but they listened to her. Bly was confident and intense, and her ideas impressed them. So did the sad tale of the lost purse.

The publisher and editor agreed to consider her story ideas. They gave her $25 to live on, which would be considered an advance on her salary if they eventually hired her. Three days later, they sent for her. They would give her the opportunity to develop one of her ideas. If the article was successful, she would have a job.

The story that Pulitzer and Cockerill wanted, however, would be anything but easy for Bly to get. They had selected her most daring proposal: In order to find out about the treatment of patients at the notorious asylum on Blackwell's Island, she would feign insanity and have herself committed. Pulitzer and Cockerill assured her that they would have her released after a week—although they were not certain how they would achieve this. During that week, however, Bly would have no contact with the outside world.

Her first challenge would be to assume the characteristics of insanity convincingly enough to fool the doctors at the asylum. The second would be to summon the courage she would need to face the terrifying ordeal of spending a week on Blackwell's Island. But Bly was determined to go through with her plan. If she carried it out, she would have a job. And, more important to Bly, she would help what she termed "the most helpless of God's creatures, the insane."

After spending fruitless months seeking work, a desperate Nellie Bly visited the World *and refused to leave without seeing the publisher. Her boldness won her a trial assignment.*

In 1887 Nellie Bly undertook a daring reportorial assignment: To discover how New York City handled its mentally ill, she feigned insanity and had herself committed to an asylum.

SIX

Inside the Madhouse

Blackwell's Island has been re-named Roosevelt Island and is now a popular residential area studded with high-rise apartment buildings and neatly manicured parks. But in 1887, when Nellie Bly ventured there to report on the treatment of the insane for the *World*, the small East River island housed a vast asylum for mentally ill people whose families were too poor to pay for their care. Sixteen hundred women were housed in the women's ward, most of them against their will. The public knew little about the place, though rumors of hellish conditions occasionally filtered out. Bly resolved to penetrate the mystery and uncover the truth.

"I was to chronicle faithfully the experiences I underwent," Bly wrote later, "and when once within the walls of the asylum to find out and describe its inside workings, which are always so effectually hidden by white-capped nurses, as well as by bolts and bars." Cockerill, her editor at the *World*, had warned her against sensationalizing her reports. "Write up things as you find them, good or bad," he said. "Give praise or blame as you think best, and the truth all the time."

The night before her masquerade was to begin, Bly was unable to sleep. Instead, she prepared herself for the part she was to play. Sometimes, she knew, madness takes the form of irrational fears. In order to simulate this state, she read ghost stories late into the night. She rehearsed before a mirror, pulling her long hair down around her face and staring vacantly at her reflection. She filled a notebook with nonsensical scribbling. As she worked herself into the proper mood, chills

NELLIE PRACTICES INSANITY AT HOME.

This illustration from Nellie Bly's Ten Days in a Madhouse *shows Bly preparing to act the part of a mentally disturbed woman.*

raced up and down her back. She was terrified.

The next morning, with 73 cents in her pocket, Bly made her way to the Temporary Home for Females, a cheap boardinghouse. She assumed a faraway look, rang the bell, introduced herself as Nellie Brown—the name she and her allies at the *World* had agreed to—and asked for a room. She paid the 30-cent fee in advance, then another 30 cents for a drab dinner she could hardly choke down.

In the lodging house's shabby, crowded parlor, Bly took note of the other residents. As she later described the scene, most were working women with no other place to go. One woman sat reading, ignoring her noisy young son. Another repeatedly fell asleep and awakened herself with her own snoring. Other women sat idly or worked at knitting and lacework. The doorbell rang over and over, signaling the arrival of women, some with children, who needed shelter for the night. An unkempt housemaid flitted in and out, endlessly singing snatches of songs. Bly found the boardinghouse noisy, irritating, and depressing. How miserable to have to call such a place home, she thought.

Bly sat in the parlor for hours, doing nothing and speaking to no one. As she later reported, after a few hours her strange behavior drew the attention of the home's proprietor, Mrs. Stanard. "What is wrong with you?" she asked. "Have you some sorrow or trouble?"

Bly assumed her role. "Yes, everything is so sad," she said.

"We all have our troubles, but we get over them in time," replied the matron. "What kind of work are you trying to get? Would you like to be a nurse for children and wear a nice white cap?"

Bly put her handkerchief to her face to hide a smile. "I never worked. I don't know how," she replied, in muffled tones.

"But you must learn," Stanard urged. "All these women here work."

"Do they?" asked Bly in a low whisper. "Why, they look horrible to me; just like crazy women. I am so afraid of them. There are so many crazy people

A resident of a "working girl's home" partakes of a frugal meal. Bly began her undercover odyssey at the Temporary Home for Females, a similarly desolate boarding house.

about, and one can never tell what they would do. Then there are so many murders committed, and the police never catch the murderers." Bly concluded this strange speech with a dramatic sob. She laughed to herself as poor Mrs. Stanard quickly took her leave.

Bly continued to sit in the boarding-house parlor. She punctuated her silence only to remark occasionally that the other women in the house all looked crazy. As it grew later and she refused to go to bed, her behavior began to upset the other women. "Poor loon!" said one. "She will murder us all before morning," cried another. Bly's roommate refused to sleep in the same room with "that crazy woman."

Bly sat up all night, fully dressed, staring blankly at the parlor wall. To every question she replied that she had forgotten everything and had a terrible headache that would not go away. Over and over, she repeated that she was a foreign traveler waiting for her trunks to arrive.

It was a long night for everyone at the Temporary Home for Females. A woman down the hall woke screaming, saying she had dreamed that the crazy foreign woman chased her with a knife. Bly kept her vigil in the parlor, staying awake by studying the armies of cockroaches scampering about the room.

In the morning Bly resumed her refrain about the lost trunks and refused to leave the house. Desperate, Mrs. Stanard finally sent for the police. Two officers escorted Bly to the stationhouse and then to the courthouse. According to Bly's later account, her feigned insanity failed to win her any sympathy. "If she don't come along quietly I will drag her through the streets," one of her escorts announced brusquely. A band of ragged children joined the procession, shouting, "Where did you get her, cop?"

At the courthouse a kindly looking judge, struck by her genteel appearance, questioned "Miss Brown" thoroughly. The reporter, feigning a Spanish accent, told him she was from Cuba, but she could not remember anything else. She had only a few pennies left and was alone. The judge called a doctor, who ordered her removed to Bellevue, a public hospital.

Bly was taken to the wing reserved for the mentally disturbed. As she waited to be examined, she heard blood-chilling shrieks coming from another room. Trying to maintain her composure, she spoke to several other patients sitting nearby. One unfortunate woman told Bly that she had become sick from overwork and had been transferred to Bellevue when her family ran out of funds to keep her at a private hospital. At Bellevue, she had been mistakenly assigned to the mental ward and now found herself unable to get out. "The doctors refuse to listen to me," she told Bly.

Bly sat waiting a long time. A nurse

Rats scurry over sleeping patients at Bellevue Hospital. Posing as a disoriented woman named Nellie Brown, Bly was taken to Bellevue for psychiatric examination.

came by and ordered her to remove her hat, pulling it off herself when Bly did not respond. Finally a doctor arrived to question her. After spending just a few minutes with Bly, he pronounced her "positively demented" and "a hopeless case."

That night she was assigned a hard bed in an ice-cold chamber with barred windows. Sleep was impossible.

The ambulance gong sounded through the night, nurses stood in the hall talking in loud tones, and screams issued from the male ward nearby. At six o'clock in the morning, Bly was ordered from bed and fed watery broth. This routine was repeated for several nights.

Bly was seen by more doctors, who confirmed the initial diagnosis. By now the papers were filled with reports of a mysterious gentlewoman about to be taken to Blackwell's Island. Swarms of reporters descended on the hospital to get the story. Bly avoided them, terrified that her true identity would be discovered. But her secret stayed intact, and the *World*'s rival papers identified her only as "the Beautiful Wreck" and "the insane girl who has no memory of her past."

On Sunday, September 25, 1887, Nellie Bly was committed to Blackwell's Island. She had been diagnosed as suffering from "dementia with delusions of persecution." Her nails were cut to the painful quick, presumably so

that they could not be used as weapons. She was taken to the docks, where a rough attendant smelling of whiskey escorted her and several others onto a dirty boat bound for the asylum.

Once she arrived on the island, Bly was hurried into a pavilion, again to face a panel of medical experts. As she waited, she listened indignantly as the doctors casually questioned the other new arrivals. Some of them seemed as sane as Bly herself, but the medical authorities seemed to take no notice. A sobbing, bewildered German immigrant, for example, was given no opportunity to make her case. Bly thought it likely that she had been

When Bly arrived at the insane asylum at Blackwell's Island (shown here), she was prepared for primitive conditions. But the grim realities she found there far exceeded her expectations.

confined to the asylum because she spoke little English and could not make herself understood. She later wrote indignantly that "criminals are given every chance to prove their innocence. These poor, overworked girls are convicted after a few trifling questions."

By this time, Bly had resolved to act normally except to refuse to tell who she was or where she lived. She was examined by another doctor, who was more interested in flirting with the nurse than in questioning his patient. "I am not sick and I do not want to stay here," said Bly firmly. But the doctor ignored her and added his signature to all the others in her file.

Bly marched with the other inmates through drafty cold halls to an unin-viting dining room. Supper was revolting: thick bread with rancid butter, coppery-flavored tea, and prunes. Then the patients were ushered into an unheated bathroom where they were stripped and scrubbed with cold water and a dirty rag. "My teeth chattered and my limbs were goose-fleshed and blue with cold," Bly reported later. Three buckets of icy water were flung over her head as a rinse. "I think I experienced some of the sensations of a drowning person," she wrote. "For once, I did look insane."

Dripping wet, she was dressed in a light flannel slip, rushed into a room, and put into bed. She noticed that one of the other recent arrivals, a frail woman suffering from a high fever, was shivering in her damp, thin slip. As she

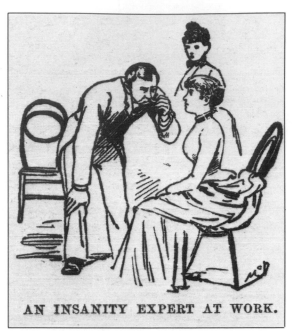

AN INSANITY EXPERT AT WORK.

This illustration from Ten Days in a Madhouse *shows Bly undergoing an examination. She later reported that most of the doctors at Blackwell's Island were careless in their diagnoses.*

reported in her book *Ten Days in a Madhouse*, Bly asked a nurse to get the young woman a dry nightgown.

"We don't have nightgowns here," the nurse responded gruffly. "This is charity."

"But the city pays to keep up these places," Bly pointed out, "and pays people like you to be kind to the unfortunates brought here."

Bly's independent attitude infuriated the nurse. "You'd better understand something," she barked. "You don't need to expect kindness here, for you won't get it. Understand?"

Damp and chilly between a slippery oilcloth-backed sheet and a too-small blanket, the reporter lay awake picturing the horrors that would ensue if a fire broke out in the asylum. Each room's door was locked separately from the outside, and the windows were heavily barred, blocking any escape. Few of the 300 women imprisoned in the building, Bly thought grimly, would survive a fire.

The following days brought more indignities and inhumane treatment. A single coarse towel was shared by dozens of patients, even though a few seemed to be suffering from contagious skin diseases. The food was unwholesome and unpalatable. The patients were assigned the hard work of cleaning the institution or were expected to sit quietly for hours on stiff benches. At the time, little was known about treating the insane, and minimal care was the rule. Bly had expected Blackwell's Island to be a place of hopelessness and despair. Nonetheless, the viciousness and negligence of many asylum employees deeply shocked her. For the most part, patients were ignored by the doctors, and some of the nurses actually seemed to take pleasure in tormenting their charges. Bly was appalled as she saw the mental and physical health of many of the patients decline day by day under the asylum's cruel regimen. She would later charge that the treatment patients received on Blackwell's

Asylum inmates eat a meager dinner. Bly found that patients at Blackwell's Island were served tiny portions of unpalatable food while the staff enjoyed hearty meals.

Island could drive perfectly sane individuals mad.

Aside from physical labor such as floor scrubbing, the only exercise permitted the inmates was supervised walks on the grounds. Bly's first impression of the landscaped yards as a place of comfort and beauty quickly evaporated. The grounds were overrun by inmates, many of them babbling nonsense or confined in straitjackets, who were virtually ignored by the staff. She was especially horrified by the sight of 50 filthy women roped together and made to walk in single file. These, it was whispered, were the violently insane patients who were confined to a section of the asylum called "The Lodge." Bly noticed that some of the residents of this ward had injuries such as broken bones and black eyes. Rumor had it that these wounds were inflicted not by inmates but by the staff. Frightened by these reports, Bly resolved to stay clear of The Lodge.

Days passed, and still Nellie Bly heard nothing of her release. The reporter had long since abandoned the fiction of being insane herself. Each time a doctor made a rare visit to the ward, she would ask to be released, speak rationally, and beg them to try any test of sanity on her. But, as she wrote later, "the insane asylum on Blackwell's Island is a human rat-trap. It is easy to get in, but once there it is impossible to get out."

At last, after ten hellish days, Bly was informed that "friends" had arranged for her release. The newspaper had finally played its hand. Nellie Bly was a free woman again.

"I left the insane ward with pleasure and regret," she wrote, "pleasure that I was once more able to enjoy the free breath of heaven; regret that I could not have brought with me some of the unfortunate women who lived and suffered with me, and who, I am con-

Neglected inmates crowd a ward at Blackwell's Island. After the World *printed Bly's articles on the institution, reforms were enacted and the staff-to-patient ratio improved dramatically.*

vinced, are just as sane as I was, and now am."

Bly's exposé of Blackwell's Island hit New York like a bombshell. Thousands bought the *World* to find out, for the first time, what really went on at the notorious asylum. After reading Bly's graphic account of her shocking experiences, many of them joined her in angrily calling for reform. A grand jury

was convened to investigate the institution on Blackwell's Island. Bly testified before the commission, then accompanied the jurors on a fact-finding mission.

Her second trip to the island proved vastly different from her first. The hospital administrators, aware that an investigation was going on, had hastily rectified the worst abuses. The asylum seemed cleaner, the food was more wholesome and abundant, and the inmates were dressed in clean clothing. Some of the patients Bly had suspected were sane were no longer at the institution. Because of these changes and deceptions, she worried that the grand jury would not believe her charges. But the court agreed with Bly that conditions had to be improved on Blackwell's Island. Three million dollars was appropriated to increase the staff and improve the living conditions of the inmates.

Bly had done what she had set out to do. She had fooled New York's medical establishment and gone undercover in an insane asylum. She had exposed the injustices she found there and successfully worked for reform. Her exposé was picked up across the country, and dozens of investigations into public and private mental hospitals ensued.

An institutionalized woman rattles the bars of her cell. Although she was initially afraid of the patients, Bly soon found that she had more to fear from abusive staff members.

Impressed with her courage and her idealism — not to mention her ability to sell newspapers—Joseph Pulitzer and John Cockerill offered Bly a job. At last, she was a reporter for the New York *World*. Nellie Bly had passed the test.

As Nellie Bly had hoped, her startling 1887 exposé on the treatment of the insane won her a job on New York's most progressive major paper, the World.

SEVEN

Nell of the *World*

With the publication of the first of her articles on Blackwell's Island, Nellie Bly had literally become an overnight sensation in New York. Immensely proud of its new reporter, the *World* promised its readers that she would continue to champion the poor and the powerless. Bly wasted no time before starting work on her next big exposé. Always interested in the plight of the "working girl," she made the rounds of employment agencies, posing as a naive young woman looking for work. She had heard that many of these companies preyed on desperate or inexperienced job seekers.

At her first stop, the Germania Servants' Agency, Bly was required to pay a registration fee before anyone would speak to her. She listened with growing indignation as the proprietor made inappropriate comments about her appearance. Although she told him she had never worked before, he insisted on advertising her as an experienced laundress. When even this fraudulent claim failed to find her a job, the agency refused to refund her fee.

Bly fared no better at the employment bureau of Mrs. L. Seely. Once again, a fee was exacted up front—this was a common scam, she learned. She waited with 50 other hopefuls in a small, dingy room. One by one, many of the women around her were turned down for jobs. Most of these decisions were based solely on the whim of the employment agents. Some were sent away for being too tall or too heavy, while others were recommended for jobs for which they were totally unqualified.

Bly angrily described her findings in the *World*. She pointed out that employment agencies that took advantage of would-be employees often cheated employers as well. By lying about a job candidate's experience and character, these organizations often provided incompetent or dishonest labor.

As she had done in Pittsburgh, Bly investigated the lot of female factory workers by hiring on alongside them. She wrote a series of exposés on the workplaces of these laborers, including one on a box-making workshop. "I did not find the work difficult to learn, but rather disagreeable," she wrote of this operation. "The room was not ventilated, and the paste and glue were very offensive. In case of fire there was practically no escape."

Bly, as a trainee in the box factory, earned nothing for her labors. After two weeks, she was promised, her weekly wage would be approximately $2.50, depending on how fast she worked. One young woman, considered a success by her peers, had worked her way up to $5 per week after 11 years in box factories. But as she confided to Bly, even this relatively high salary left her very little to live on. "I pay out $3.50 for board, and my wash bill at the least is 75 cents," she told Bly. "Can anyone expect a woman to dress on what remains?" Others Bly met were helping support families with their meager pay. As she had before, Bly transformed the stories of

A woman chooses between two eager candidates at an employment agency. Posing as a job seeker, Bly found that some of these companies cheated both employers and prospective employees.

This cartoon depicting the evils of the British sweatshop system was equally applicable to the New York factories that Bly exposed in her articles for the World.

these workers into an eloquent plea for labor reform.

Bly turned her attention to other issues as well, often disguising herself to carry out her bold investigations. For one reporting expedition, Bly sought out "fallen women"—those who had turned to crime to support themselves—to find out what caused their downfall. Her sympathetic articles blamed the plight of these women on desperate circumstances, alcoholism, and unhappy family situations, not on the women themselves. Another time, Bly posed as a penniless innocent. As she had suspected, she was quickly approached by a man who made his living by duping or coercing young women into prostitution. After she exposed his racket, he was seen about town no more.

No corner of the city was too seamy, no institution too crooked, no stunt too dangerous, for the determined Nellie Bly. Legend has it she even threw herself off a Hudson River ferry to test the efficiency of its rescue crew. Another time, she asked a friend to accuse her of robbery so that she could investigate prison conditions. Once she was cleared and back at the *World* office, she wrote up shocking tales of leering jailhouse guards, crude treatment, and a corrupt court official who

Standing amidst discarded shells, women shuck oysters. As a World *reporter, Bly continued to expose dangerous and inhumane working conditions.*

offered to bribe a judge to buy her freedom. Her front-page revelations led to the strict segregation of male and female prisoners and to the replacement of male officers by the city's first police matrons, who would be as-

signed to frisk incoming woman prisoners.

Bly was interested in political as well as social reform. One of her first attacks in this area was leveled at Edward R. Phelps, a powerful lobbyist in Albany, the capital of New York state. For years Phelps had been suspected of graft and crookedness, even of being connected with the criminal underworld. But Phelps was slick and canny, and no one had ever been able to prove anything against him.

Nellie Bly vowed to unmask Edward Phelps, even though she had been warned that if he found out what she was up to, the consequences might be fatal. The journalist carefully formulated a plan. A bill to restrict the sale of potentially dangerous over-the-counter medicines was up for a vote in the New York State legislature. Bly would masquerade as the wife of a medicine manufacturer and offer to bribe Phelps to use his influence to stop the bill. Donning her best clothes, Bly paid him a visit at an Albany hotel. Practically in tears, she told Phelps that her husband's business would be ruined if this bill were passed into law. She offered him $2,000 if he could convince local politicians to defeat the bill.

Tricked by Bly's story, Phelps told her he could kill or save any bill he chose. He showed her the names of half a dozen state representatives. "I can buy the lot for one thousand dollars," he bragged. Bly struck a deal with Phelps and asked for a receipt. Then, on the pretext of having left her checkbook in her room, she fled with the receipt in her hand. She had not only scooped every political reporter

A woman contemplates drowning herself in this engraving entitled The Street-Girl's End. *Bly wrote several sympathetic pieces on women who had turned to crime because of desperate circumstances.*

in New York, she had finally gotten incriminating evidence on one of the state's most notorious influence peddlers.

Bly's front-page story ran in the April 1, 1888, issue of the *World*, which

Nellie Bly tames a tiger, the symbol of the influential political organization known as Tammany Hall. In 1888 Bly took on Tammany Hall when she exposed corrupt lobbyist Edward Phelps.

quickly sold out. THE KING OF THE LOBBY, shouted the headline. Smaller type proclaimed: "Edward R. Phelps Caught in a Neatly Laid Trap. Nellie Bly's Interesting Experiences in Albany." The piece ran with a cartoon drawing of Phelps, a crown on his head, his feet up on a desk, his chair surrounded by bags of money. Under this picture was printed a sarcastic poem:

For I'm a Pirate King!
I'm in the lobby ring!
Oh! what an uproarious,
Jolly and glorious
Biz for a Pirate King!

Bly told the whole sordid story of Phelps's offer to kill the patent-medicine bill. The public demanded an explanation, and Albany's "Pirate King" was indicted and forced to admit his deal with Bly. The careers of several state legislators whose votes and influence had been up for sale abruptly ended after other investigations. Once again, justice—and Nellie Bly—had triumphed.

Switching her focus from the unscrupulous to the idealistic, Bly interviewed lawyer, suffragist, and social reformer Belva Lockwood for the *World*. Lockwood had run for the U.S. presidency on the National Equal Rights party ticket in 1884 and was making a second attempt when Bly met with her in 1888. The two women had a searching discussion. Lockwood told Bly of the difficulties a woman faced in gaining admission to law school and being accepted in the legal profession. She also spoke of her hope that women would soon win basic rights, such as the right to vote. At a time when many people considered feminists "hussies" or "unnatural women," Bly wrote an evenhanded piece on Lockwood that may have caused some of her readers to reconsider their views.

Nellie Bly soon had an impressive collection of articles to her credit. Her eye-opening pieces continued to serve as important tools for New York's reformers, and her concern for the poor and downtrodden made her the dar-

"Prairie" Rose Henderson rides a bucking bronco at a New York City rodeo. For one of her lighter articles, Bly profiled several traveling horsewomen in the World.

This 1890 photograph shows a New York slum. Bly was passionately concerned with the city's poor and often visited these areas to report on conditions there.

ling of the reading public. She visited slum districts and vividly described the squalid conditions she found there: crowded, unsanitary tenements; grinding poverty and illness; single faucets shared by a dozen families. She spent a day at a soup kitchen, then called for more food services for the poor, especially children. Posing as an invalid, Bly inspected the free dispensaries to see what sort of medical care the city gave its poor. She applauded self-sacrificing doctors who worked at the clinics for low pay and exposed those who were incompetent or preyed on the destitute. During this expedition Bly narrowly escaped from a doctor who was about to remove her tonsils—without anesthesia—to cure her sore throat.

The *World*'s most celebrated reporter also addressed less serious topics, delighting her readers with tales of thrilling adventure and comical escapades. She interviewed "the girls of the wild west," horsewomen who performed on the rodeo circuit. She went up in a hot-air balloon. She talked her way into a place in a chorus line and had the grace to laugh at her clumsy dancing—and the courage to describe it to her 200,000 readers.

The *World* protected Bly's identity so she could proceed anonymously, a key element in the success of her undercover work. This anonymity also made for good drama. It kept New York speculating on the person behind the byline. Many believed that the intrepid Nellie Bly could only be a brilliant male reporter, or even a team of journalists. At the time few Americans could imagine a young woman still in her twenties accomplishing so much. But the best was yet to come. In 1889 she would amaze millions by performing a feat that had long been considered strictly the province of fiction.

This photograph was taken on January 25, 1890—the day Nellie Bly made history by completing her 72-day trip around the world. Her time far surpassed all previous records.

EIGHT

Around the World

Coming up with ideas for the week's work usually posed no great challenge to Nellie Bly. New York burst with possibilities, and none were beyond consideration. But one autumn Sunday in 1888, Bly found herself racking her brains for a new topic. At three o'clock the next morning she was still tossing and turning in her bed without a single fresh notion. As she later described this pivotal night, she finally said to herself in exasperation, "I wish I was at the other end of the earth!"

Now there was an original thought. "And why not?" Bly said to herself. "I need a vacation; why not take a trip around the world?" She recalled one of her favorite novels, Jules Verne's popular fantasy *Around the World in Eighty Days*. Bly wondered if it was really possible to circle the globe in that amount of time, as Verne's hero Phin-

eas Fogg had done. Still mulling over this thought, she finally fell asleep.

On Monday an excited Nellie Bly stopped into the office of a steamship company and studied the schedules. When she arrived at the *World*, she confronted her managing editor, Jules Chambers. "I want to go around the world!" she announced. "I think I can beat Phineas Fogg's record. May I try it?"

Bly was dismayed when Chambers informed her that someone had already suggested the idea and that the newspaper intended to send a man. "In the first place you are a woman and would need a protector," he told her. "Even if it were possible for you to travel alone you would need to carry so much baggage that it would detain you in making rapid changes. No one but a man can do this."

The World.

CIRCULATION GUARANTEED GREATER THAN THAT OF ANY TWO OTHER AMERICAN NEWSPAPERS COMBINED.

CIRCULATION BOOKS OPEN TO ALL.

CIRCULATION PER DAY DURING LAST 7 MONTHS, 340,167 COPIES.

12 PAGES.   NEW YORK, THURSDAY, NOVEMBER 14, 1889.   12 PAGES.

THE LINES OF TRAVEL TO BE FOLLOWED BY "THE WORLD'S" FLYING REPRESENTATIVE.

This map depicting Bly's proposed route appeared in the World *on the day she began her trip, November 14, 1889.*

"Very well," replied the reporter angrily. "Start the man and I'll start the same day for some other newspaper and beat him."

Chambers sized up his furious employee. "I believe you would," he said. By the time their meeting ended, he promised that if anyone made a globe-spanning journey for the *World*, it would be Nellie Bly.

But for nearly a year it looked as if the trip would not be made. Bly got involved in other projects and, hearing nothing more from her boss, put her ambitious idea aside. Then one cold, rainy evening her editor summoned her to his office. "Can you start around the world the day after tomorrow?" he asked.

"I can start this minute," she answered, her heart pounding with excitement.

At first glance, Bly's travel plans seem tame by today's standards. An 80-day trip around the globe sounds quite leisurely in an age of jet planes and space shuttles. But in Bly's time transportation involved steamships, slow trains, and stagecoaches. As she planned her itinerary, she faced a number of daunting unknowns. The schedule of the mail train from Calais, France, to Brindisi, Italy, was uncertain. Arrivals and departures for the ships she had to rely on for much of her transportation varied with the weather conditions and were sometimes delayed for days. And the weather might indeed be severe, Bly knew, because she would be traveling in the Southern Hemisphere at a time when that region was often beset with monsoons and storms.

Bly would set off with a ticket to London, some cash, and a letter of credit. Making the remaining connections would be up to her. She would be alone at train stations and in port towns. By 19th-century standards, her plan was quite unconventional—and potentially dangerous.

Her hasty preparations for the journey were unconventional as well. In Bly's day women usually traveled with full wardrobes packed in heavy trunks. But since she could not rely on porters and her schedule might depend on hairbreadth connections, she resolved to travel light. She had a fashionable dressmaker stitch up a sturdy blue

Jules Verne, above, wrote Around the World in Eighty Days, *the book that inspired Bly's journey. Verne applauded Bly's efforts to break the fictional record set by his character Phineas Fogg.*

wool traveling outfit. Another tailor made her a lightweight dress for hotter climates. She bought a plaid ankle-length overcoat, a silk raincoat, and a practical Sherlock Holmes–type gillie cap.

Packing her luggage—a single crocodile "gripsack," or suitcase—was a challenge. She stuffed in her spartan travel wardrobe, a toothbrush, a bankbook, slippers, veils to protect her face against soot and sun, toilet articles, writing implements, needles and thread, handkerchiefs, a jar of cold cream, two hats, a blazer, some changes of underwear, and a silk bodice. In the end she had to sacrifice the new summer dress.

On November 14, 1889, the morning she was to depart, Bly had a bad case of the jitters. She feared that another journalist would take the same trip and beat her time or that she would not be able to make the trip in under 80 days to beat Phineas Fogg's imaginary record. On top of everything else, she was exhausted. Consumed by her work, Bly had not taken a vacation in almost three years, and she was plagued by recurrent headaches. Trying to ignore these problems, she put on her lucky thumb ring and bid farewell to the friends and colleagues who had come to see her off. Then she steamed out of a New Jersey harbor on the German ship *Augusta Victoria*.

The *World*'s headlines that day were calculated to spark enthusiasm about Bly's journey:

AROUND THE WORLD!
A CONTINOUS TRIP WHICH WILL GIRDLE THE SPINNING GLOBE

NELLIE BLY TO MAKE AN UNEQUALLED RAPID—TRANSIT RECORD

NOW 30,000 MILES IN A RUSH!

CAN JULES VERNE'S GREAT DREAM BE REDUCED TO ACTUAL FACT?

Bly made the initial leg of her trip aboard this steamship, the Augusta Victoria. *The first night out the ship hit violent storms that gave Bly second thoughts about her plans.*

The story went on to explain Nellie Bly's latest exploit to the paper's readers. It detailed her plans and described her preparations: "Miss Bly starts out with a gripsack for the longest journey known to mankind—she knows no such word as fail, and will add another to her list of triumphs—circumnavigation of the globe. The *World* today undertakes the task of turning a dream into a reality."

But far from the excitement and grand rhetoric that emanated from the *World*'s offices in New York, Nellie Bly was facing the first difficult trial of her journey. As she later confessed, she was stricken with severe seasickness, to the vast amusement of the other passengers aboard the *Augusta Victoria*. "And she's going around the world!" one man sneered as she rushed to the side rail and leaned over.

Bly went to bed and woke refreshed the next morning. She learned that the night had been rough for everyone: The sea had been stormy, and two sailors were washed overboard. Yet after this dreadful beginning, the crossing to England proceeded without serious incident. Bly had plenty of time to amuse herself by observing her fellow passengers.

She would later describe some of the most colorful passengers in *Nellie Bly's Book*, a chronicle of her journey. There was a man who took his pulse after every meal, another who counted the number of steps he took pacing the deck. A little terrier named Home Sweet Home spent the voyage in the quarters of the ship's butcher, occasioning black humor over the contents of the sausages. One woman slept in her clothes so that she would be found "decent" if the ship went down during the night.

When the *Augusta Victoria* docked in Southampton, England, Bly was met by the British correspondent for the *World*. The two of them then traveled to London together. He told her that Monsieur and Madame Jules Verne had cabled the paper's office, inviting her to visit them in France. Bly was thrilled. Verne was one of the era's most popular writers, and of course, the character he created had been the inspiration for her trip. Not only was she personally interested in meeting Verne, she knew the detour would make good copy for her readers back home. But it *was* a detour, and she was racing against the clock. To keep her schedule, she would have to do without sleep for two nights.

After an English breakfast and a cup of coffee, with barely a glance at Westminster Abbey and the Houses of Parliament, Bly left London on a mail train. She was accompanied by her English colleague, who spoke French and could act as interpreter during the next leg of her voyage. Together the two reporters made the chilly crossing of the English Channel. At Boulogne-sur-Mer, France, they caught the train

During her travels Nellie Bly was not always able to cable back reports, so the World staff kept readers' interest up with articles and promotions such as this board game.

to Amiens, where the Vernes had their estate.

Bly was immediately impressed by the writer and his elegant wife. Verne inquired about life in the United States, then asked about her trip. Bly described her itinerary, and the two discussed the ways it differed from that of Phineas Fogg. Although Verne had his doubts that she could beat his fictional character, his hopes were with Bly. "If you do it in seventy-nine days, I shall applaud with both hands," said Verne, toasting her. "Good luck, Nellie Bly."

It was time to leave. The *World*'s star reporter arrived in Calais exhausted. Much as she longed for a long rest in a comfortable bed, she knew she could not afford the time. After midnight she boarded a mail train that would take her through Italy to Brindisi via a picturesque route along the Adriatic Sea.

Bly arrived at Brindisi two hours late, worried that she had missed the ship she hoped to take to Egypt. Luckily, the *Augusta Victoria* was still in port. Bly checked in, dropped her suitcase off in her cabin, then hurriedly ran back down the gangplank to send a quick cable back to her colleagues at the *World*. To her astonishment, the clerk at the telegraph office had never heard of a far-off place called New York. Bly waited nervously as he slowly figured out the cost of the cable. Her brief message sent news and greetings. Then she dashed back to the pier and

Veiled women and turbaned men were some of the novel sights that Bly described to her readers after her arrival in Egypt.

onto the boat with less than five minutes to spare.

As Bly later recounted the tale, the passage to Port Said, Egypt, was a peculiar one. From the stewardess who ordered the late-rising Bly to get out of bed to the captain who ignored his passengers, the ship's crew was uniformly rude. The band that played at dinner was the worst the reporter had ever heard—perhaps because the

From a vantage point on a temple balcony, worshipers view the gardens in Kandy, Ceylon (now Sri Lanka). Marooned for five days, Bly saw more of Ceylon than she did of most other points on her itinerary.

musicians were also working as dish-washers. Meanwhile, a rumor circulated that Bly was an eccentric heiress, traveling with only a hairbrush and a bankbook. This led to an offer of marriage from a fortune hunter who hastily retreated when he learned Bly's true identity. Another man, a dandy who had 19 trunks aboard ship, also proposed to her. He told the astonished Bly that he had been searching all his life for a woman who could travel without much luggage.

On November 27 the *Victoria* docked at Port Said to refuel. Bly took advan-tage of the stopover to tour the city and observe its residents. Back in New York, her audience would read of the beggars, street markets, and heavily veiled women she saw in Egypt.

The ship continued on to Aden, in Yemen, then Columbo, Ceylon (now Sri Lanka), where she impatiently waited five days for a ship east. The sun was burning hot as Bly explored these places, marveling at the exotic scenes. She attended the theater and watched street performers. Bly studied the local foods, clothing, and customs. She took a *jinrikisha*, a two-wheeled wagon hauled by a man on foot and saw relics of the Buddha, exotic temples, and the beautiful gardens of Peradeniya. She found the British flag waving everywhere she went on this leg of the trip, for she was traveling through what was then part of the vast British Empire.

Whenever she could, Bly cabled reports home. In between her telegrams, daily columns were written by the newspaper staff in order to maintain interest in her journey. Bly's saga was building the paper's circulation dramatically, and the *World* milked her story for all it was worth. Reporters described the history, geography, and weather of the areas she was passing through. They imagined the dangers she might run into and speculated on the adventures she might have. One of these stories, for instance, was headlined: SOME OF THE QUEER THINGS NELLIE BLY WILL SEE DURING HER STAY IN JAPAN. To further pique reader interest, the newspaper printed a game board showing the stops Bly would make so that the public could chart her progress at home. The *World* sponsored a contest that would award a free trip to Europe to the reader who came closest to guessing the exact day and hour of Nellie Bly's return home. Other papers picked up the news. People across the United States—and the world—were avidly following her progress.

From Ceylon, a small British ship named the *Oriental* took Bly to Penang (now Malaysia) for a few hours' stop. By December 18 she was sightseeing in Singapore, an island in the South China Sea. There she was especially struck by the sight of a funeral procession. Escorting a scarlet-draped casket were dozens of attendants bearing roast pigs and Chinese lanterns, playing cymbals and fifes. On her way back to the ship, she was enchanted by a street peddler's monkey and bought him as a mascot for her journey home.

On the way to Hong Kong, the *Oriental* steamed through a violent monsoon. Water filled the passengers' cabins, and great waves washed over

A Chinese jinrikisha *driver pulls a passenger through city streets. Of all the forms of transportation Nellie Bly used on her around-the-world trip, this was certainly the most exotic.*

87

A FREE TRIP TO EUROPE !

(Including first-class transatlantic passages, railroad fares and hotel bills)

TO THE PERSON WHO FIRST MAKES
THE NEAREST GUESS
AS TO THE
EXACT TIME OF NELLIE BLY'S TOUR.

NEXT SUNDAY'S WORLD
WILL PRINT A
NELLIE BLY BLANK BALLOT.

Upon this blank ballot all guesses must be made, the ballots being cut out and mailed to THE SUNDAY WORLD. Guesses not made on THE WORLD blanks cannot compete. Only one guess can be made on a single blank, but any reader of THE SUNDAY WORLD can send in as many guesses as he or she pleases, by procuring extra blanks from extra copies of THE SUNDAY WORLD. Full particulars Sunday. There will be an extraordinary demand for these blank ballots, and you should not fail to

Order Next SUNDAY'S WORLD at Once.

Promotions such as this contest kept interest in Bly's trip high—and helped sell thousands of copies of the New York World.

the decks. By this time Bly was an experienced sailor, and she took the storm in stride. "The terrible swell of the sea during the monsoon was the most beautiful thing I ever saw," Bly wrote. "I would sit breathless on deck watching the bow of the ship standing upright on a wave, then dash headlong down as if intending to carry us to the bottom."

The small ship reached Hong Kong on December 23. Proud to be carrying their illustrious passenger into the British colony two days ahead of schedule, the crew fired a cannon as their craft entered the shimmering bay. By now, thinking of little else besides the time she was making, Bly hurried to the steamship office to book the first passage to Japan. She had just marked off her 39th day of travel, and she was elated with how well things were going despite the loss of 5 days in Columbo.

But the booking agent pulled her aside. "You are going to be beaten," he said. "The day you left New York another woman started out to beat your time, and she's going to do it." This competitor, the man explained, was a reporter for another New York publication. She had left Hong Kong three days before, heading in the opposite direction, with easy connections ahead. Worse, he told Bly, the boat for Japan was not due to leave for five days. Another five-day delay awaited her at Yokohama. And because of the season, it was likely that her trip across the Pacific would be a slow one.

"That is rather hard, isn't it," said Bly quietly, forcing a smile but overwhelmed by this bad news.

A despairing Nellie Bly checked into her hotel. Because she did not have a change of clothes, she discouraged prospective hosts who offered to give dinners and receptions in her honor. The way things were going, she

A pagoda looms in the background of this Canton, China, harbor. Bly's vivid descriptions enabled readers back home to envision the scenes she saw on her whirlwind trip.

doubted that celebrations were in order, anyway.

On Christmas Day she arrived in Canton, China, where she spent a somber holiday. She visited a "ghastly" leper colony, a jail where she saw torture implements, and a Buddhist shrine known as the Temple of the Dead. The only bright spot came as she passed the American consulate and saw her native flag waving in the wind. Until that moment, she later

reported, she had not known how homesick she had been.

Bly was in Japan by New Year's Day, 1890. The *World* reporter's confidence and good spirits returned, and she wrote enthusiastically about the nation, which she felt blended the best of European and Oriental culture. She found Japanese men polite, the women elegant, the art impressive. She ate rice and eel, explored the temples, and prowled the curio shops. "In short," she wrote in her dispatch to New York, "I found nothing but what delighted the finer senses while in Japan."

As she boarded the *Oceanic* for her voyage back to the United States across the Pacific, Bly was heartened by a sign placed over the engine by the chief engineer: "For Nellie Bly, We'll win or die!" The ship steamed out of Yokohama in perfect weather. On the third day of the crossing, however, a storm rose, and Bly grew melancholy. "If I fail, I will never return to New York," the reporter despondently told her shipmates. "It's hopeless!"

Sympathetic to Bly's plight, the captain ordered the ship's boilers stoked, and the crew raced to make up the lost time. Finally, the *Oceanic* reached San Francisco, California. More trouble was

When Bly's ship, the Oriental, *steamed into Hong Kong harbor (left) on Day 39 of her trip, the crew fired off a cannon in honor of their illustrious passenger.*

NELLIE BLY

These drawings depict the highlights of the triumphant conclusion of Bly's trip. Her journey ended in Jersey City, New Jersey, where she was greeted by thousands of well-wishers.

to come, however. The ship had left its passengers' bills of health in Japan. All aboard faced two weeks of quarantine before they could leave the boat.

Desperate, Bly threatened to jump overboard and swim. Her threat must have been taken seriously, because that very day a tugboat arrived to carry her to San Francisco. As the tug steamed off, the quarantine doctor called to her from the deck. He had

forgotten to examine her tongue, he shouted to her, and she could not land until he had. The exuberant Nellie Bly, with her monkey beside her, stuck out her tongue and waved farewell. It was January 21, the 68th day of her trip, and she was back in America.

The *World* had a special train waiting in San Francisco to rush her across the country. Bly's trip across the continent was a blur of telegrams, cheers, and congratulations. Wherever her train stopped, she was greeted as a returning hero. Flags flew along the route, bands played, and crowds strained to catch a glimpse of her. The Chicago Press Club held a reception in her honor. The welcome in her old hometown, Pittsburgh, was especially enthusiastic. On the day of Bly's arrival there, the *Dispatch* devoted its entire front page to its most famous alumna.

On January 25, 1890, Bly leapt from her train at the Jersey City station, which was packed with thousands of well-wishers. A great yell went up from the crowd. Cannons boomed the news of her arrival. Nellie Bly was home. She had traveled 24,899 miles, circling the globe in 72 days. It was a new world record.

This jubilant cartoon appeared on the front page of the New York World *on January 26, 1890, the day after Bly's return from her astounding 72-day, 6-hour trip.*

Although the investigative journalism she pursued before and after her trip was the prime focus of her career, Nellie Bly was most celebrated for her globe-trotting feat.

NINE

Triumphs and Trials

On January 26, 1890, the day after Nellie Bly's return, the New York *World*'s front page exclaimed: FATHER TIME OUTDONE! EVEN IMAGINATION'S RECORD PALES BEFORE THE PERFORMANCE OF "THE WORLD'S" GLOBE-CIRCLER. She had left New York a local celebrity and returned an international hero. Bly received a flurry of congratulatory telegrams, including one from author Jules Verne. Songs were written about her daring exploits. A racehorse was named after her. Bly's picture was used to advertise products from cigars to soap. In contrast, Elizabeth Bisland, who had raced Bly and lost the competition by four days, was quickly forgotten.

Exhausted, Nellie Bly gave up her duties at the *World* to enjoy a well-earned rest. She was hardly inactive, however. She compiled her notes and observations into a best-selling volume entitled *Nellie Bly's Book: Around the World in 72 Days*. She went on speaking tours and wrote for a variety of publications. She was the best-known reporter of the day, and possibly the most highly paid. In 1890, at the peak of her fame, she earned $25,000, a monumental sum at the time.

Bly reveled in her success. The crusading reporter, the friend of the poor and powerless, also enjoyed comfort. She could don a ragged costume and embrace danger and discomfort, but afterward she wanted a hot bath and elegant clothes, fine food, white gloves, and beautiful things. Now that she was a wealthy woman, she bought property in an exclusive summer colony, Millionaire's Row, in Brooklyn's Sheepshead Bay. There she hoped to relax and, as she wrote her friend Erasmus

NELLIE BLY, ON THE FLY.

When Nellie Bly went on the fly,
To show what courage dared to try,
She made the startled world contess
Men don't monopolize success.

Schenck's Mandrake Pills

Cure all Bilious and Liver Complaints.

Following her return from her ground-breaking trip, Bly found herself an international celebrity. Her name and image were used to advertise a dizzying array of products.

Wilson, try her hand at writing a novel.

But as time went on, the temptation of a front page byline proved too strong for Bly to resist. In 1893 she returned to the *World* with renewed vigor. Her stories were as emotional, moralistic, and sensational as ever.

Bly was given her own features column. She introduced it this way: "This is all my own. Herein every Sunday I may say all I please and what I please." Her first subject was typically controversial. She interviewed the notorious Emma Goldman, an anarchist, who believed that laws and government should be abolished. At the time of their meeting, Goldman was in a New York City prison awaiting trial for allegedly inciting unemployed men and women to steal bread. Many saw "Red Emma" as a dangerous threat to society. But although Bly disagreed with Goldman's ideas, she was convinced of her commitment to assisting the poor and dubbed her "a modern Joan of Arc."

Bly's energy seemed boundless. She worked alongside Salvation Army volunteers and penned an inspiring story that sparked an outpouring of donations to the charitable organization. She exposed a famous mind reader as a fraud. Bly interviewed convicted murderers to get their side of the story. She even spent a night in a haunted house waiting for a ghost to show up.

Nellie Bly traveled to the town of Pullman, outside Chicago, Illinois, to cover the violent railroad strike of 1894. Her view of the situation changed drastically after she visited the so-called model community that inventor and businessman George Pullman had built for the workers who manufactured his train cars. She looked behind

A determined-looking Bly appeared on the cover of Nellie Bly's Book: Around the World in 72 Days. *The volume was published in 1890, the year she completed her journey.*

the showy public buildings that surrounded the train station and discovered that they hid poor and cramped dwellings owned by the company and rented out at high prices. Although many newspapers printed reports that painted the strikers as irresponsible lawbreakers, Bly maintained that they had real grievances. She was shocked

by the violence used by federal troops that Pullman had called in to break the strike.

Bly shared her conclusions with her readers on July 7: "I went to Chicago bitterly set against the strikers. From what I could tell, the inhabitants of Pullman's model town had no reason to complain and I intended to denounce them in my column. But before I'd been there half a day, I became the bitterest striker of them all." Bly was dismayed when the strike was finally broken on July 13, 1894.

The following year Bly traveled to Nebraska to report on the plight of a different set of workers: ranchers suffering from the ill effects of two years of summer droughts and harsh winters. She interviewed dozens of farmers and wrote several pieces on their desperate situation. Then, with the *World*'s backing, she set up a relief committee to aid the ranchers. Her assignment completed, she boarded a train bound for Chicago.

It was on this train that Bly met Robert L. Seaman, a wealthy 72-year-old Brooklyn industrialist. He had made his fortune founding the Iron Clad Manufacturing Company, one of the nation's largest hardware enterprises. Seaman was distinguished, sophisticated, intelligent—and captivated by his traveling companion. By the time they reached Chicago, the two had begun a romance. Little is known about their courtship, but in

NELLIE BLY'S
COLUMN.
-------◆-------
This is all my own.
Herein every Sunday I may say all I
please and what I please.

*After taking time off for lecture tours
and a variety of writing projects, Nellie
Bly returned to full-time newspaper
journalism in 1893, when she began a
weekly features column.*

April 1895, Bly's newspaper published
an announcement that startled many:

> The readers of the Sunday *World* will
> surely be interested to know that Nellie
> Bly is married. She is now Mrs. Robert
> Seaman. Her marriage, like most of the
> other important events in Nellie Bly's
> life, was out of the ordinary. She met
> her husband on the train, on the way to
> Chicago, only a few days before she be-
> came a bride.

Bly had rebuffed many suitors in the
past, and her sudden marriage bewildered both her friends and her public.
Some speculated that the 30-year-old
reporter had finally decided to give

marriage a try, others believed that she
had simply finally found the right man
in Robert Seaman. But her husband's
age and wealth sparked a good deal of
malicious gossip in some circles. Although Bly herself was quite well off,
she was labeled a fortune hunter.

But Nellie Bly was not one to listen
to critics. Blithely ignoring public opinion, she abandoned her newspaper
career to assume a new role. As Mrs.
Elizabeth Cochrane Seaman, she en-
tertained in grand style in the elegant
Manhattan home she and her husband
shared. She also staged elaborate par-
ties at their sprawling estate in Catskill,
New York. A niece and nephew who
came to live with her for long stretches
marveled at the servants, the cham-
pagne, and the rich furnishings that
now surrounded their Aunt Pink.

Bly did not limit herself to the role of
rich hostess. As a journalist, she had
often focused on the relationship between employers and workers; now, as
the wife of a factory owner, she had the
opportunity to put her ideas into practice. Her husband slowly withdrew
from the everyday affairs of his business, and Bly began to fill his shoes.
With her help, the company nearly
quadrupled its business in the next
few years.

Robert Seaman died of a heart attack
on March 11, 1904. When Bly recovered
from the shock of his passing, she
found herself a millionaire and the
owner of the Iron Clad Manufacturing

Company. Determined to run the business herself, she turned down offers to buy out her share in the company.

Nellie Bly applied herself to her new role with characteristic energy. The company was profitable and employed 800 workers, but she still considered many of its methods antiquated. Bly now spent seven days a week at the factory, figuring out better ways to turn sheet metal into a myriad of items, from enameled washtubs to industrial drums. She was the first to develop and mass-produce steel barrels in the United States, and her innovation was popular with the burgeoning oil and chemical industries. Within years she nearly doubled Iron Clad's employee rolls and set up a new business that could make 1,000 steel drums a day. The American Steel Barrel Company was the largest in its field, with sales of $1 million per year. Once again, Nellie Bly was breaking ground in a traditionally male world.

Although she was now a factory owner, Bly did not forget her previous convictions. The former crusader for equality and justice increased wages and improved working conditions. She paid women the same as men and provided health care to all her workers and their families.

"What has become of our one-time little friend, Nellie Bly?" wrote her old colleague, "Quiet Observer" Erasmus Wilson, on May 16, 1906. "Oh, she is all right. She is worth about $5 million

Bly profiled American anarchist Emma Goldman (pictured) in 1893, when Goldman was jailed on charges of inciting workers to violence. Bly's portrait of the radical social reformer was sympathetic.

dollars, and has been so taken up with the management of a large manufacturing plant, working 1,500 men and turning out thousands of car loads of finished products annually that she simply has had no time to write. She has always been given to doing things that others could not do or feared to undertake."

But trouble was ahead for Nellie Bly. A fire in the Iron Clad's storage facilities destroyed $10,000 worth of stock in one day. A salesman whom she fired for rudeness sued her for $25,000. Finally in 1912 she discovered that several employees had embezzled money from the company over the years. Bly's world collapsed.

Suddenly creditors were clamoring at the gates. Bly promised to pay them. "And I'll keep on making steel barrels til I die," she swore. But she found she could not pay off her debts, and the Iron Clad Manufacturing Company filed for bankruptcy in 1913. Bly was dragged into court for a long, bitter legal battle. Day after day, lawyers for her creditors—in collusion with some disgruntled former employees—slandered her, charged her with perjury, and argued that the assets of the steel-

THE IRON CLAD FACTORIES
ARE THE LARGEST
Of their kind and are owned exclusively
by
✳ NELLIE BLY
The only woman in the world
personally managing
Industries of such a magnitude
NATIONAL BOTTLERS' CONVENTION
CLEVELAND, OHIO
OCTOBER 15, 16 and 17, 1901

Bly's 1895 marriage to industrialist Robert Seaman surprised both her friends and her readers. Many were even more shocked when she took over Seaman's business after his death nine years later.

barrel company Bly had created should be turned over to pay the Iron Clad's debts. As her legal troubles became public, Bly was castigated as a failure. This, she said, hurt her most of all. She told a reporter for the *New York Times* that part of her problems arose from the skepticism and hostility she encountered as a woman in the male-dominated world of business. In July 1914, worn out and her fortune exhausted, the 50-year-old Bly left for Austria.

She had planned to rest and recover there for just a few weeks, but an international crisis drastically altered her plans. On July 28, Austria-Hungary declared war on Serbia. Within weeks, most of Europe was engaged in the bloody conflict that became known as World War I. Finding herself caught up in the war, Bly decided to begin report-

Railroad employees menace a train guarded by armed federal troops during the Pullman strike of 1894. Unlike most journalists of the time, the crusading Nellie Bly sided with the workers.

ing again. As America's first woman correspondent in the war, she sent dispatches home to the New York *Evening Journal*, which was edited by her friend Arthur Brisbane, himself a legend in newspaper journalism.

World War I ended in 1918, a year after the United States entered the conflict, and Bly returned to America soon afterward. The courts at last had vindicated her. Though its assets were greatly reduced, the Iron Clad Manufacturing Company was hers. But this judgment failed to end her troubles. In an attempt to protect her property during the war in Europe, Bly had signed it over to a wealthy Austrian businessman, Oscar Bondy. But since he was a citizen of a country that had been at war with the United States, her property, including some of her stock in Iron Clad, was confiscated by the American government under the Alien Custodians' Act. Bly's financial status had also suffered as the result of family rivalries. During her stay in Europe her mother, who was her legal representative, and her brother, whom she had supported for many years, had sold much of her Iron Clad stock and had kept the proceeds.

Despite her adversity, Nellie Bly was still an imposing figure who dressed in fashionable silks and furs. Her dark eyes still flashed with intensity, and she retained the energetic air of her youth. "Nellie Bly still overpowers one with her striking personality," noted a

The first woman to cover the World War I battlefront, Bly interviews an Austrian officer. She traveled to Austria after her manufacturing business failed and was stranded there when war broke out.

reporter for the *Brooklyn Eagle* upon her return from Europe.

Behind the mask, though, was a bitter woman who had lost everything she had worked for. To Erasmus Wilson, she wrote of her family's betrayal, her sadness at losing her company, and her frustrating financial difficulties. "I have exactly $3.65 and a trunk full of Paris evening dresses," she wrote her old friend. "These I shall sell to replenish the $3.65—that is if I can."

At the age of 55, Nellie Bly found that she had to start all over again. As she

Evening Journal *editor Arthur Brisbane, above, printed Bly's war reports during her sojourn in Europe. After her return in 1919, he hired her as a regular columnist.*

had more than 30 years before, she turned to the newspaper world. Brisbane at the *Evening Journal* offered a job, and she eagerly accepted. On May 24, 1919, the *Journal* introduced its newest columnist in a front-page spread. The headline for Bly's story, on a poor man who made good, might have applied to the author herself: A MAN MAY BE DOWN, BUT HE'S NEVER OUT. "This is the first of a series of articles which Miss Bly will write," explained a note to the *Journal*'s readers. "Her subjects will be various, and to each she will bring the human sympathy

and keen insight for which she is so well known."

Yet there was to be no dramatic comeback for the veteran reporter. Twenty-five years had passed since she had been a newsroom regular, and times had changed. A new generation of journalists had been forged by World War I. Newspaper sensationalism was out of style. So were the emotional, opinionated articles that had been Bly's trademark. Although they still faced prejudice, women were no longer curiosities in the field. Bly, the trailblazer, was all but forgotten. Her colleagues paid little attention to the mysterious figure in the hat and dark veil as she made her way to her private office at the *Journal*.

But Bly was used to pursuing good stories and pleasing her readers—no matter what her skeptical peers thought. She had done it in her youth, and she continued on this course in her middle age. Bly continued to champion the cause of working women, and she covered the Republican National Convention of 1920 with notable insight. She was especially devoted to the cause of the abandoned children who roamed New York's streets. She wrote a series of articles that told the stories of these youngsters and appealed to her readers for help. Until families were found to adopt them, she cared for many of these children herself in her two-room suite in the Hotel McAlpin.

Bly met this boy while working as an advocate for the hundreds of New York City children abandoned by their parents. Through her columns, she found homes for many of these youngsters.

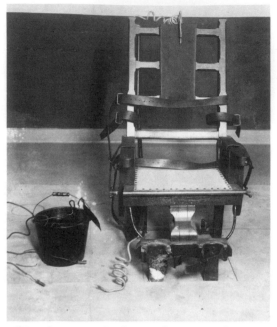

This photograph shows the type of electric chair used in 1920, the year Bly witnessed an execution and wrote an impassioned plea against capital punishment.

It was in her role as children's advocate that Nellie Bly made national headlines again. In December 1919 an abandoned baby was found with a note pinned to him. "For the love of Mike," it read, "somebody take this kid. He is one too much for the family. Give him to Nellie Bly of the New York *Journal*. He is seven months old and as healthy as they make 'em. Can't afford him on the price of milk they are charging today. There are others I am trying to support."

Bly accepted this charge and was taking steps to adopt the infant when a woman named Mrs. August Wentz came forward. She claimed the child as her own kidnapped baby and took him home, but the story did not end there. A 24-year-old widow named Lena Lisa insisted that she was the infant's real mother. She said she had grown desperate trying to support two children on the $12-per-week pay she earned making artificial flowers. After an investigation that was followed on New York's front pages, her son, Harry, was finally returned to her.

Nellie Bly's last great scoop came in January 1920 when she became the first woman in decades to witness a public execution in New York State. She traveled to Sing Sing prison, where Gordon Hamby, a convicted murderer, was to be electrocuted. Bly, passionately opposed to capital punishment, had corresponded with Hamby. She visited the convict in his cell and gave him his last cigarette. As the current was turned on, Bly, who sat as far from the electric chair as possible, shut her eyes.

Her account in the next day's paper rang with all her old indignation. Dramatically headlined HORRIBLE! HORRIBLE! HORRIBLE!, her story charged that capital punishment represented the worst kind of hypocrisy. "Hamby is dead," she wrote. "The law has been carried out—presumably the law is satisfied. Thou Shalt Not Kill. Was that Commandment meant alone for Hamby? Or did it mean all of us?"

Two years later, on January 14, 1922, Nellie Bly was stricken with pneumonia. The progress of her illness was swift. On January 27 she passed away at the age of 58. Although her reputation had diminished during the last few decades of her life, journalists across the country recorded the passing of one of their own. Her obituary in the New York *World* recalled her triumphs for the paper, including her dazzling trip around the globe and her courageous undercover work on Blackwell's Island. The Pittsburgh *Dispatch*, the publication that launched her career, noted that "she was considered the best reporter in America." Her reputation has not been eclipsed by time. More than a half century after her death, the New York Press Club erected a new tombstone over her grave in a ceremony that commemorated her fascinating life and tremendous accomplishments.

"What shall we do with our girls?" young Elizabeth Cochrane had wondered in 1885. Dissatisfied with the usual answers, she created a new persona—Nellie Bly—who addressed that question with a unique blend of exuberance and concern. She showed that women could do anything they cared to, including excel at "man's work." She not only paved the way for the women who would follow in her footsteps, she also launched a dramatic new kind of journalism based on firsthand experience. Opinionated and

On January 27, 1922, Nellie Bly died after a lifetime of stirring consciences and breaking precedents. Honoring one of their own, the New York Press Club erected this monument over her grave in 1978.

direct, she became an effective voice for social reform and the nemesis of lawbreakers, scoundrels, and those who exploited the poor and helpless.

As biographer Mignon Rittenhouse said of Bly, "She bettered the world for others while fulfilling her own destiny." Bly attacked life with spirit, determination, and heart. These qualities carried her into dangerous, unfamiliar, and exotic realms. Triumphing over the obstacles she found, Nellie Bly proved that adventure, achievement, and independence are within a woman's reach.

FURTHER READING

Baker, Nina Brown. *Nellie Bly.* New York: Holt, Rinehart, and Winston, 1956.

Cochrane, Elizabeth. *Nellie Bly's Book: Around the World in 72 Days.* New York: The Pictorial Weeklies Company, 1890.

————. *Six Months in Mexico.* New York: J. W. Lovell, 1888.

————. *Ten Days in a Madhouse.* New York: N. L. Munro, 1887.

Noble, Iris. *Nellie Bly: First Woman Reporter.* New York: Messner, 1956.

Rittenhouse, Mignon. *The Amazing Nellie Bly.* New York: Dutton, 1956.

Ross, Isabel. *Charmers and Cranks.* New York: Harper & Brothers, 1936.

————. *Ladies of the Press.* New York: Harper & Row, 1965.

Verne, Jules. *Around the World in Eighty Days.* New York: Bantam, 1984.

CHRONOLOGY

May 5, 1864	Elizabeth Cochran born in Cochran's Mills, Pennsylvania
July 1870	Her father, Michael Cochran, dies
1879	Cochran attends the Indiana State Normal School in Indiana, Pennsylvania
Jan. 1885	Begins working as a reporter at the Pittsburgh *Dispatch*
Feb. 1, 1885	Publishes "Mad Marriages," her first article to carry the "Nellie Bly" byline
1885	Writes a series of articles on working women
1886	Travels to Mexico as a foreign correspondent for the Pittsburgh *Dispatch*
1887	Returns to the United States; settles in New York
	Wins a job at the New York *World* after having herself committed to uncover conditions at a city insane asylum
	Writes *Ten Days in a Madhouse*
1888	Publishes *Six Months in Mexico*
April 1, 1888	Exposes corrupt lobbyist Edward Phelps by going undercover for the *World*
Jan. 25, 1890	Completes a round-the-world trip in a record-breaking 72 days
1890	Leaves the *World* to pursue other writing projects, including her third book, *Nellie Bly's Book: Around the World in 72 days*
1893	Returns to the New York *World* as a features columnist
1894	Covers the Pullman Railroad strike
April 1895	Marries industrialist Robert Seaman
1904	Robert Seaman dies; Bly takes charge of his company, Iron Clad Manufacturing
1913	After a series of legal and financial hardships the Iron Clad Manufacturing Company files for bankruptcy
July 1914	Bly travels to Austria, where she is trapped by the outbreak of World War I
1914–17	Works as a war correspondent for the New York *Evening Journal*
1919	Returns to the United States; continues to write for the New York *Evening Journal*
Jan. 27, 1922	Nellie Bly dies of pneumonia

INDEX

PICTURE CREDITS

The Bettmann Archive: pp. 12, 16, 17, 28, 30, 35, 36, 38, 42, 43, 44, 46, 50, 53, 54, 55, 59, 65, 66, 67, 76, 92;   Carnegie Library of Pittsburgh: pp. 14, 15, 22, 26, 32, 37, 100;   Culver Pictures: pp. 33, 45, 47, 48, 49, 61, 70, 71, 72, 73, 75, 81, 82, 85, 86, 87, 89, 90, 91, 99, 100, 102, 104;   Foster Hall Collection of the Stephen Foster Memorial, University of Pittsburgh: p. 31;   Indiana University of Pennsylvania Library: p. 25;   International Museum of Photography at George Eastman House; p. 52;   Lankerd Thomas Genealogical Library/ Armstrong County, Pennsylvania Historical Museum Society, Inc./ Preston Campbell: p. 23;   Library of Congress: pp. 2, 18, 20, 78, 84;   Museum of the City of New York: pp. 62, 63;   New-York Historical Society: pp. 19, 80, 96;   New York *Journal American,* Harvey Ransom Humanities Research Center/Apollo Memorial Library/Apollo, Pennsylvania: p. 24;   New York Public Library, Astor, Lenox and Tilden Foundations: pp. 58, 64, 74, 88, 97, 98;   Muriel Nussbaum: p. 105;   Pittsburgh *Post Gazette:* p. 56; UPI/Bettmann Newsphotos: pp. 40, 68, 93, 94, 101

ACKNOWLEDGEMENT

The author wishes to thank Muriel Nussbaum for the use of her research collection. Ms. Nussbaum is an author and actress whose one-woman show, "Byline: Nellie Bly," has been performed at the Smithsonian Institute.

Elizabeth Ehrlich is a writer and editor. She is currently social issues editor of *Business Week* magazine. As a journalist, she has written about social policy, education, energy, economics, business, finance, and the arts. She received a B.A. in history and economics from the University of Michigan at Ann Arbor. Married, she has one child and lives in New York City.

Matina S. Horner is president of Radcliffe College and associate professor of psychology and social relations at Harvard University. She is best known for her studies of women's motivation, achievement, and personality development. Dr. Horner serves on several national boards and advisory councils, including those of the National Science Foundation, Time Inc., and the Women's Research and Education Institute. She earned her B.A. from Bryn Mawr College and Ph.D. from the University of Michigan, and holds honorary degrees from many colleges and universities, including Mount Holyoke, Smith, Tufts, and the University of Pennsylvania.